Lucid Dreaming

An Exemplary Spiritual Expedition For Overcoming Stress, And Anxiety While Enhancing Sleep Quality

(An Informative Manual For Harnessing The Potential Of Lucid Dreaming)

Maxwell Butler

TABLE OF CONTENT

Eleven Indicators That You Possess The Ability Of Lucid Dreaming 1

The Path 38

Lucid Dreaming Training 45

Dream Yoga 66

The Dream You Loved 70

The Advantages Of Lucid Dreaming 84

The History Of Lucid Dreaming 103

Collaborating With Your Spiritual Guides 129

Select Your Framework Based On Your Conviction 152

The Roles And Significance Of Lucid Dreaming ... 155

Eleven Indicators That You Possess The Ability Of Lucid Dreaming

Certain individuals possess an innate ability to naturally engage in lucid dreaming. I have encountered an individual of such nature and derive immense pleasure in listening to his anecdotes pertaining to his lifelong ability to exercise control over his dreams, dating back to his early childhood. Many individuals, similar to ourselves, must put effort into acquiring the skill of becoming proficient in lucid dreaming. Irrespective of the position one holds within the spectrum, presented herein are eleven indicators that demonstrate one's readiness to assume authority over their aspirations and convert them into a vivid reality.

You have intense daydreams. Intense denotes a striking and unrestrained quality, wherein one readily drifts into such vivid reveries. Furthermore, you possess the ability to engage in vivid and elaborate forms of imagination.

You possess the capacity to awaken spontaneously on several occasions throughout the week, without the assistance of an alarm.

It is feasible for you to readily recollect your dreams on most evenings. This holds significant importance in the realm of lucid dreaming. Additionally, possessing a strong capacity for recall will enhance the vividness of your dreams.

Your dreams frequently exhibit a heightened level of intensity.

You have previously experienced episodes of lucid dreaming.

In previous instances, you have exhibited the ability to rouse yourself from a distressing dream.

You engage in meditation on multiple occasions throughout the week, possibly even on a daily basis.

You consistently maintain a dream journal and engage in frequent discussions pertaining to your dreams. This could potentially be an internal dialogue. Certainly, if you feel reluctant to disclose the contents of your dreams to your colleagues, that is entirely unnecessary. Maintaining a dream journal proves beneficial for the part of engaging in conversation as it enables one to recite its contents orally.

You frequently engage in gameplay of first person perspective video games. Extensive research conducted over the course of several years has indicated that the act of engaging with simulated realities offered by video games during one's waking hours significantly influences the content and quality of one's dream experiences during the night.

You may encounter sensations of disembodiment or episodes of sleep paralysis. Although those may be perceived as intimidating, they are indeed the initial stages of a profoundly vivid dream. It is comparatively infrequent, yet nevertheless a lucid dream.

You possess a pronounced inclination towards exerting control over your dreams. Verbally expressing your intention to experience a lucid dream has the potential to be sufficient in inducing such a state. Dreams are composed of the amalgamation of one's thoughts and intentions. Placing that before entering into sleep enhances the probability of experiencing a lucid dream.

You might have encountered any or possibly even a singular instance of these. It is not mandatory to have fulfilled each item on this list in order to achieve lucid dreaming. With diligent practice and the incorporation of meditation, you will promptly attain the ability to experience lucid dreaming.

Chapter 2– Defining Dreams

Dreams, broadly speaking, can be characterized as the visual representations, perceptions, and cognitive processes that transpire during periods of slumber. All individuals possess the capacity for dreaming, albeit often unable to recollect the contents of these experiences. In the initial instant upon awakening from a remarkable dream, every aspect appears exceedingly distinct. The fragrances and emotions are readily accessible with a mere touch. Subsequently, within a fleeting moment, it has vanished. At times, we are able to recollect a few particulars from a dream.

There exists a distinction between an ordinary dream and the state of lucid dreaming. The capacity to experience lucid dreaming is characterized by an individual's deliberate awareness and control over the content and trajectory of their dreams. One not only has the ability to recollect the hues, sensations, textures, and aromas, but is also capable of exercising mastery over these elements and integrating them harmoniously. In the context of a usual dream, our ability to exert control is absent. Occasionally, instances of disorder, terror, jubilation, and even nocturnal fantasies can arise. Lucid dreaming entails exercising conscious control over the unfolding events. Put simply, lucid dreaming refers to the state of being conscious that one is experiencing a dream while in the rapid eye movement (REM) phase of sleep, the stage in which all dreams are known to transpire. (During the state of sleep, there is a swift movement of the eyes accompanied by the temporary inability of the muscles to move)

Frequently, upon awakening from an exceptionally delightful dream, we ponder the reasons behind our inability to retain those cherished memories. One notable aspect of lucid dreaming is that it enables the retention of vivid memories and the accurate recollection of events that transpired during the dream. It represents a wholly novel realm awaiting thorough exploration. During the state of unconsciousness, which is sleep, the five senses become inactive within dreams. Envision the experience of possessing those faculties within the realms of your dreams. The senses of touch, olfaction, vision, auditory perception, and even gustation can be encountered through the phenomenon of lucid dreaming.

Lucid dreaming is not easily achievable by simply going to bed and immediately transitioning into this state. It is a complex procedure that necessitates time and effort to comprehensively comprehend, cultivate, and effectively set into motion. There are no adverse implications associated with lucid dreaming. In the event of an incorrect action, the world shall not implode, nor shall it witness the opening of a mystical portal unleashing invincible creatures. It's your world. Your senses. Your journey. It constitutes a realm in which one can discover valuable artifacts, perform operatic acts, compose highly successful literary works, or engage in slumber alongside esteemed actors/actresses. In a realm devoid of constraints, the potentialities become infinite.

One might consider conceptualizing their physical form as resembling a glove. Whilst in a state of wakefulness, one remains bound by the finite capacities of their physical form. It is not possible to engage in aerial transport outside of a aircraft, nor can one partake in space exploration unless possessing the credentials and training of an astronaut. Our physical selves are what tether us to reality, and there is no inherent flaw in that. It is an intrinsic aspect of the human condition and the experience of existence, both of which are imbued with profound beauty. Lucid dreaming provides us with the opportunity to engage in actions that were previously deemed implausible. Within the realm of dreams, we are liberated from limitations. The handwear is removed, and we are liberated to pursue our aspirations without constraint.

In the final analysis, there are innumerable possibilities. During the state of slumber, an inherent bond is forged to the marvelous existence that is one's own being. You have unbounded potential. Maintaining clarity of mind during sleep allows for the commencement of exploration towards one's desired aspirations. You construct the existence you aspired to forge for yourself, gradually harnessing those remarkable potentials and manifesting them in your conscious reality.

The 5th Lucidness
Strategies for Cultivating Intense Amorous Connections

To captivate a charming suitor through love, effectively aligning with your distinct temperament and personal development, it is imperative to gain a comprehensive understanding of the qualities that allure these potential partners to your innermost consciousness. In the absence of this invaluable knowledge, we are compelled to contemplate the perplexing inquiry of what might be amiss within myself.

One is compelled to ponder why individuals with a deficiency in affection consistently gravitate towards my presence, causing me to question the inexplicable ease with which I repel the captivating suitors I yearn for the most.

If you find yourself weary of consistently attracting stagnant relationships centered solely around physical appearance or financial status, it suggests that you are emanating misguided energy.

"If one is unable to remain authentic to oneself, what adversity
Is anyone in your vicinity currently in possession of
to remain loyal and honest towards you?

Charles Rivers

You will need to enact a significant transformation in your lifestyle. As we mature into adulthood and assume the role of working-class individuals, we adopt a persona that does not align with our genuine conscious or unconscious psyche. The majority of individuals have become significantly disconnected from their true selves since their early years, to the extent that even their relatives and cherished ones find it challenging to comprehend them.

Developing Your Authentic Self

Each of us maintains a distinct yet genuine existence within the confines of our residences; however, this need not remain the status quo. To fully partake in life's myriad blessings, it is imperative that you reconnect with your authentic self. In the event that one does not enact personal transformation, a perpetual cycle of attracting undesired outcomes shall persistently prevail.

I refrain from asserting derogatory labels towards individuals, yet I maintain the conviction that each of us possesses a unique essence that gravitates towards particular types of individuals and circumstances in our existence. After consistently experiencing this recurring feedback cycle throughout our lives, we have come to truly perceive ourselves as the individuals and situations that are naturally drawn to us. However, each one of us has, at some point in our lives, either watched romantic movies or engaged with similar literary works.

Within the realm of these literary works and cinematic productions, the protagonist invariably attains the affections of their desired romantic partner. why is that? In every single one of those literary works and films, I can assure you that you have never encountered an introductory line resembling: "The Hero or Heroine Where, Great Followers of People." No, what you have indeed read or witnessed is the portrayal of the protagonist as an individual possessed with a deep zeal for life and affection.

This idealistic notion epitomizes the desire that resides within all individuals for certain qualities in others, even though they may inadvertently disregard or deny such qualities within themselves. Every individual is inherently born with an innate zest for living, yet as life unfolds, we tend to forfeit this fervor in exchange for a preoccupation with eventual retirement.

What messages am I conveying?
Suitable and Unsuitable Partners?

In this exercise, it is imperative that you authentically present yourself in order to earnestly attract genuine love. To truly embody our authentic selves, it is necessary to embark upon the introspective journey of self-discovery, with the fundamental question in mind: "What constitutes my true identity?" Our essence extends far beyond the superficialities of physical presentation, encompassing a complex multidimensionality that mere grooming, personal care, or fashionable attire cannot encapsulate. The reflection we encounter each morning in the mirror does not accurately portray how others perceive us, particularly those who are drawn to us on a physical, intellectual, and emotional level.

Your physiological composition might be attempting to convey specific visual representations that you are attempting to project, yet simultaneously, your subconscious is casting a favorable or unfavorable judgment on this affiliation. The subconscious mind possesses a distinct nature from that of the physical body and volition. It has the capacity to hinder matters pertaining to the heart that are in discord with one's aura. People that are interested in us see our unconscious projection of our inner selves long before they see our sexual looks.

To gain insight into the perspective of the individuals you are seeking to attract and eliminate personal bias, refrain from relying on the opinions of your acquaintances. There exists a substantial disparity between the perspectives of a friend and those of a potential partner, whether for one night or a lifetime. With friendship; like attracts. In light of the fact that you bear striking similarities to your friend in various aspects, it is indicative that they have developed an affinity towards you. In matters of love, similarity repels while attracting divergent awareness.

Allow me to elucidate the reason behind this. This phenomenon can be attributed to the fact that those who are drawn to you perceive something in your consciousness that is absent in their own. You share an equal level of attraction towards them due to their possession of a strength that happens to align with your primary weakness. For instance, if one tends to be reserved in their communication style, they might find themselves drawn to a forward-thinking individual who is expressive.

You are drawn to that individual due to their unwavering courage to express their thoughts openly, disregarding the audience present. They are drawn to you due to your aura of strength, tempered by a tranquil and patient demeanor, which embodies the qualities they deeply desire. Although both of you may form relationships with individuals beyond the confines of your residence, individuals who embody your values and beliefs, it is imperative to comprehend that such associations alone shall not bring about your personal fulfillment.

In light of the fact that individuals are caught off guard, their level of awareness becomes completely deficient. A companion can only enhance what is already present within you, whereas an adversary can enhance areas where you lack, provided you grant them the opportunity to do so. The full realization of one's intellect, which leads to clarity, necessitates the engagement of both cerebral hemispheres, rather than solely relying on the same hemisphere as one's friend.

Certainly, it is the natural inclination for the subconscious to be drawn to its opposite in the realm of romantic relationships, hence giving rise to the phenomenon of opposites attracting. Please bear in mind that you will inevitably draw towards you that which you lack within yourself. Therefore, if you wish to avoid attracting individuals who are determined to change you, it is imperative that you address and rectify any personal issues beforehand.

In general, it is often observed that women who do not conform to prevailing beauty standards are more likely to be married in relationships. The majority of these women are likely to be shorter than five feet, in stark contrast to the models featured in magazine advertisements who often bear no resemblance to the flawlessly retouched fashion icons found on checkout counter displays.

Why is that? Similar to the aforementioned movies and literature that we discussed earlier, it is often observed that men are inclined towards women who are in need of assistance. Likewise, despite women's inherent ability to ensure their own well-being, they exhibit a preference for tall men who are inclined to protect and support them. Therefore, should one find themselves emotionally out of balance, they shall inevitably draw the interest of an individual who possesses the qualities in which they are lacking, and is inclined to rectify said insufficiencies.

The notion of "saving the damsel" in a romantic relationship, while initially endearing, becomes tedious for a woman who does not perceive herself as requiring any kind of repair or assistance. Furthermore, it becomes excessively burdensome for the man who perceives himself as having already liberated his lady by marrying her, thereby freeing her from the malevolent grip of the sorceress residing within the fortress. How can one effectively acquire their desired outcomes while minimizing undesirable results? Firstly, it is essential to assess the signal that you are transmitting. A minute ago, I told you that most people are not the person they were born to be. Hence, you are conveying an insincere indication and subsequently attracting insincere individuals.

Therefore, it is advisable to initiate self-improvement and address your deficiencies well in advance of extending an invitation to someone to enter your life. Failure to do so may result in attracting individuals who perceive themselves as the solution to your problems, reinforcing the need for repairs. Should you be seeking an individual who is open-minded, exhibits a stable financial position, and embodies the ideal lifestyle you aspire to, it is imperative that you transform yourself into that very person.

Lucid Dreaming and Meditation
B
Based on empirical evidence and personal observations, it can be concluded that there are notable parallels between lucid dreaming and the practice of meditation. Both of them entail the capacity to "possess conscious awareness of the current moment."

Mindfulness meditation entails the act of attentively observing the ongoing events as they unfold. Alternatively referred to as having conscious awareness of the immediate moment.

Mindfulness Meditation
By cultivating a deliberate practice of calming our minds, attuning ourselves to the beauty and significance of nature and our surroundings, we are creating the conditions necessary to embark

upon the realm of lucid dreaming. Unsurprisingly, a significant relationship exists between the practice of mindfulness meditation and the experience of lucid dreaming.

When engaging in meditative practice throughout the day, commonly known as "mindfulness," individuals dedicate a deliberate amount of time to observe and appreciate the intricacies of their surroundings that might have otherwise gone unrecognized.

The objective at hand is to rouse your awareness to the thoughts dwelling within your mind.

What sort of thoughts are occupying your mind? By developing a state of attentiveness towards your thoughts throughout the day, you will inherently foster an awareness of the contents of your mind during your dreams as well.

In this state of consciousness, our focus primarily revolves around the superficial layers of the conscious mind, which represents the most immediate level of engagement attainable.

Alternatively, when engaging in nocturnal or nighttime meditations, we possess the capacity to access the root itself - namely, the subconscious mind. We have been presented with the exceptional chance to confront the intellect directly.

Nocturnal Meditation/Sleep yoga
This entails a type of profound relaxation meditation wherein we strive to detach ourselves from our senses, resembling a state of slumber. For centuries, Buddhist individuals have been cognizant of the fact that the illusions experienced during dreams correspond to the illusions experienced in the state of wakefulness. They employ these methodologies to investigate the nature of existence and to ready themselves for the inevitability of mortality.

These nocturnal contemplations elicit a heightened level of transformation due to their profound depth. As we enter a state of slumber, we experience a temporary detachment from the superficial aspects of our consciousness and establish a profound connection with the collective awakened mind that we share.

As a result of this, Sleep yoga has gained recognition as an expedited route to enlightenment, a rapid pathway towards inner awakening. However, it should be noted that rapidity does not imply simplicity. It means more direct. These introspective reflections directly engage with the fundamental underpinnings of our personal encounters. According to experts in the field of depth psychology, any actions or choices made at the unconscious level carry profound implications for one's conscious existence. Even the slightest movements of tectonic plates can have substantial repercussions on the Earth's surface.

This is the reason why it holds the potential for significant transformation. The actions that you undertake in your personal sphere can have a profound impact on the external outcomes that occur.

Per Traleg Kyabgon Rinpoche, a trailblazer in the introduction of Tibetan Buddhism to Australia, the practice of dream yoga has the capacity to unlock latent possibilities that have yet to be explored, granting access to hidden reservoirs of profound insight. He shares numerous accounts wherein individuals practising dream yoga undergo remarkable transformations within the span of a single night. One has the opportunity to drift into slumber perplexed, only to awaken completely metamorphosed!!

An additional advantage of engaging in nocturnal meditations is the heightened ease with which one can develop their spiritual practices within the realm of dreams as opposed to during the daytime. This predominantly stems from the constraints imposed by our physical form throughout the course of daylight hours. During the state of dreaming, our minds achieve a state of liberation, thus opening up a multitude of potentialities.

The practice of sleep yoga and the utilization of these deeply calming nocturnal meditations have demonstrated a significant impact on the brainwave patterns of individuals, akin to the influence one experiences when in a state of sleep. As a result, you can experience a sense of rejuvenation, even in the absence of actual slumber.

Through regular practice, studies have demonstrated that it can effectively restore sleep patterns and enhance the overall quality of sleep. It should be noted that this particular form of relaxation is solely intended to enhance the quality of your sleep, rather than serving as a substitute for it.

In contrast to the more ubiquitous practice of 'yoga', sleep yoga is executed while reclining. Instead of assuming a bodily posture, one reclines in a tranquil manner while a yoga Nidra instructor serenely facilitates the entire experience.

In a manner reminiscent of mindfulness meditation, it frequently commences with a contemplation of the body, directing attention to individual parts sequentially, all the while promoting muscle relaxation and deep, intentional respiration. This is intended to facilitate the transition into a state resembling conscious sleep.

Hypnotherapy and Hypnosis
Hypnotherapy is regarded as a form of nonconventional or "complementary and alternative" therapy that is employed alongside other therapeutic modalities to address various psychological disorders.

It employs techniques such as guided relaxation, profound concentration, and focused attention to attain an elevated level of awareness often referred to as a state of trance. The individual's concentration is so acute during this state that any external activity is momentarily obfuscated or disregarded.

With the aid of a skilled practitioner, individuals have the potential to direct their concentration towards particular thoughts or activities. The recommendations embedded during the state of hypnosis can seamlessly translate into practical application in your conscious state.

Surprisingly, it is within the realm of possibility to induce self-hypnosis. You are able to effectively enter a state of heightened focus and susceptibility. In addition to inducing a sense of calm, it has the capability to facilitate the identification and alteration of undesirable habits and cognitive patterns.

In a comparable manner, the phenomenon of lucid dreaming provides the opportunity for individuals to attain a state of entrancement, wherein suggestions can be skillfully instilled within the depths of their subconscious cognition.

The primary distinction lies in the fact that lucid dreaming enables one to attain significantly greater depths. You cannot be more unconscious than being asleep.

Preliminary Foundational Activity: Recording Dreams

Dream journaling is the exercise of promptly documenting one's dreams upon awakening. This particular practice holds paramount importance as it serves as a catalyst for achieving success in the realm of lucid dreaming. Establishing this as a customary practice will facilitate enhanced recall of your dreams, enriching your ability to vividly recount them. Placing your journaling materials, such as stationary and writing utensils, adjacent to your pillow will serve as a catalyst for fostering this activity. Certain individuals may opt to record their dreams using electronic devices such as smartphones or tablets, however, based on my personal encounters, I have found that the act of manually transcribing them onto paper utilizing a pen possesses a higher degree of potency. Presented herein are several guidelines for efficacious dream journaling.

Begin by jotting down essential keywords related to your dreams

Dreams can be readily erased from memory. Despite the fact that we may experience a dream of apparent duration of 5 hours, recollecting the dream upon awakening can prove unexpectedly challenging. Making brief notations of actions, objects, locations, individuals, and so forth. The imagery that you have witnessed within your dream has the potential to enhance your recollection. Dream memory operates similarly to an internet search engine, wherein the act of entering a single keyword initiates the retrieval of relevant search results or, in this case, the recollection of additional fragments of the dream. A demonstration of this phenomenon involves the practice of capturing dream key words, which takes the following form:

Cerulean sky, picturesque natural landscape, diminutive brown poodle, absence of human presence, leisurely strolled, golden-hued foliage adorning trees, gentle zephyr, undulating path, fragrant floral fragrance, and so on.

Promptly record your dreams upon awakening in a journal

The recollection of dreams has the potential to dissipate mere minutes after the transition from sleep to wakefulness. It is crucial to promptly jot down your dream encounter. In the event that you are unable to recollect any details, kindly indicate "No Recall" in your written submission. Please note that it is crucial to develop the practice of documenting your thoughts upon awakening, regardless of whether any fragments of your dreams are remembered. In the event that no recollections of dreams are readily apparent, it would be advisable to consider traversing one's routine occurrences, encompassing activities such as meals, education, professional engagements, preferred locations, and habitual acquaintances. Engaging in a process of revisiting familiar encounters could potentially activate a recollection within one's dreaming state.

Establish Your Aspirational Objective Prior to Bedtime

Cultivate the practice of deliberately establishing a purpose or desired outcome for a fanciful experience prior to retiring for the night. Determine whether you were able to carry that intention into the realm of dreams. Instances may encompass: Endeavor to soar through the air, Seek a solution to a query that occupies your mind, Indulge in a delectable confection, Embark on a journey to a destination of choice, Engage in a meeting with a spiritual mentor, Cultivate proficiency in a chosen discipline, and so forth. Please document this intention in your journal prior to going to bed. Reiterate your desired aspiration to yourself as a positive affirmation for a duration of one minute or more.

Fourth Fundamental Practice: The Utilization of Techniques to Induce Lucid Dreams during the Nighttime Period

It is imperative that you establish a regular practice that you consistently incorporate into your bedtime routine. It is imperative for it to be identically similar, ideally occurring consistently at the identical hour every evening. The lucid dreaming practice will encompass three key elements: Purification, Lucid Dream Induction Method, and Close Down. The purification process shall commence prior to your scheduled bedtime, serving the primary purpose of inducing relaxation to both your body and mind, while simultaneously facilitating the detachment from the burdensome concerns of the day. The Lucid Dream Induction Method is employed while reclining in bed, while the Close Down is performed upon awakening in the morning.

Nevertheless, prior to implementing your nightly ritual, it is essential that you take cognizance of the arrangement of your room. I suggest positioning your bed centrally against the wall, oriented towards the doorway. Due to an unexplained rationale, this arrangement of the bed is expected to facilitate the experience of more enhanced and memorable dreams. Please ensure that you organize and declutter your room, removing any unnecessary items. Blackout curtains are highly effective in maintaining optimal darkness within the room, facilitating seamless daytime practice sessions. If the presence of excessive noise is a concern, the application of a pair of soft earbuds could be utilized as a means to mitigate some of the auditory disturbance. You desire this to serve as an environment wherein you can dedicate your complete focus towards the cultivation and mastery of lucid dreams. To achieve success in the practice of lucid dreaming, it is imperative to maintain a state of overall physical and mental well-being. Incorporate ample quantities of organic and locally procured sustenance into your dietary regimen. Reduce consumption of heavy meals prior to bedtime, and initiate a physical fitness regimen. Developing good sleep habits is crucial to achieving mastery. Retire to bed at 10:30 P.M. and rise at 6:00 A.M.

Refining the Art of Lucid Dreaming:

The purification component of your practice will comprise the following elements

Physical cleansing

Elective enhancing aid for lucid dreaming

Invocation, assertion, verification

Energy work

Physical cleansing examples:

Indulge in a steaming fragrant bath/shower/sauna, attend to personal needs, and don attire that is inherently cozy. Rest on an acupressure mat for a duration of 5 minutes. Please recline upon a grounding/earthing mat and remain in this position for a duration of 5 minutes. Take a brief stroll outdoors without any footwear, specifically on the lush grassy surface, for a duration of 5 minutes. One might consider allocating a few days to diligently engage in a water, dry, fruit, or juice fast. Research has indicated that the act of abstaining from food, commonly known as fasting, has been found to enhance the ability to remember and experience dreams with greater clarity. The utmost priority lies in attaining a state of relaxation and tranquility. One would prefer to avoid being disrupted by any form of tension.

Lucid Dreaming Supplements

This step is discretionary. This product primarily caters to inexperienced individuals seeking expedited results, or those grappling with the challenges of enhancing the intenseness and recollection of dreams necessary for inducing lucid dreaming. Mastering the art of lucid dreaming unaided by supplemental substances is imperative. One should always strive to avoid reliance on external resources.

Additional details concerning lucid dreaming supplements will be presented in the upcoming section.

Invocation, positive affirmation, pragmatic assessment:

Invoke your preferred divine entity for aid. Subsequently, proceed with your affirmations and reality checks in accordance with your usual routine. If prayer is not a part of your routine, you may choose to bypass it and proceed directly to the affirmation and reality check.

The Path

Breathe. Envision yourself traversing a splendid trail that meanders its way up a majestic mountain. The forest is lush. The hallowed trees gracefully arch above, forming a protective canopy that beckons you to venture further into the tranquil serenity of the natural world. You feel at one with the forest, as a fern gently brushes against your leg. Suddenly the path stops. Your path is obstructed by large rocks. You envisage that fellow hikers opt to change their course at this juncture. There is indeed a means available to you. You exhibit perseverance and engage in thorough observation. Miraculously, you notice the faint outline of a slender path descending. You continue. The trail leads to a plateau ahead. In the far-off distance, there lies a limpid and translucent body of water resembling an oasis amidst the arid desert surroundings. It impeccably mirrors the distant mountain. The serene tranquility of the lake's radiant blue exudes a profound sense of calmness. You experience great joy in this moment, acknowledging the divine decision for your Soul to inhabit your physical form. You sense a noticeable increase in your vibrational frequency. The fact that you are currently experiencing such tranquility is not by chance. You have made your selection and you are prepared.

You find yourself amidst a picturesque meadow adorned with an assortment of blossoming flowers, enchanting you with their delightful aroma. As you observe the graceful flutters of butterflies and the diligent buzzing of bees, you cannot help but be filled with awe. You settle into your seat to fully appreciate the breathtaking view before you. As you extend your hand to grasp a flower, you perceive the ethereal voices of the nature spirits cautioning you, "Reconsider, for the act of plucking that flower stems from the influence of the ego, which seeks to possess and govern your being." The flower would wither away. You express your gratitude to the ethereal forces of nature. As you progress forward, you assimilate the enlightened perspective of affection and impartiality.

Upon nearing a body of water, an individual observes the presence of a juvenile carrying a bag upon their shoulders. The young individual appears burdened by the considerable load of a substantial knapsack. Your intuitive inclination suggests that this is the representation of your younger self at the age of eight. You experience an internal emotional welling of tears. You greet the child. Subconsciously, you possess a desire to embrace her, and she reciprocates the sentiment. You come to the understanding that she acknowledges you as an elder iteration of her own self. A tear emerges in your eye, and your heart expands with an overwhelming surge of affection.

She places the backpack on the ground. You both embrace. You experience a sense of youthfulness - you exert pressure on yourself. You both shed tears of sheer delight as you draw near to the tranquil lake. There is a multitude of river stones, exhibiting a smooth and flat nature, rendering them optimal for the recreational activity of skimming stones upon the exceptionally calm water surface. You both engage in laughter and playful activities, observing the consequential undulations on the water's surface, subsequently settling down to take a moment of respite.

It is time to erect a flame. Sitting by the fire you ask her, "What's in the backpack?" She looks at you earnestly and says, "I must carry baggage that you have been unable to let go of." With that, Younger-You pulls out a heavy book. As you peruse the pages before you, you observe a documentation of your emotional experiences, the influence of your ego, intricate entanglements of karma, and it dawns upon you the significant burden that this luggage bears. You diligently peruse the contents of this book, selectively remove pages, and incinerate them. Young-You, overwhelmed with joy, expresses a high-pitched exclamation as a vivid purple flame emerges from the fire, rendering both of you temporarily speechless. The violet flame acts as a conduit for the absorption of negative karmic energy, subsequently facilitating the release and liberation of your present self and the version of yourself from the past. Simultaneously, you assimilate the therapeutic luminosity, thereby acquiring novel, elevated vibrational patterns. You experience the profound essence of unity, boundless love, and transformative restorative energy. You experience an unprecedented sense of tranquility. Upon awakening, it becomes evident that the presence of your younger self has vanished; nonetheless, you are reassured of her well-being and her sense of complete harmony aligns with your own.

All apprehension and skepticism have dissipated. You proclaim, without a doubt, that this is an epitome of blissful existence. You are prompted to recall the insightful statement of Carl Jung, where he affirms the necessity of embarking on a personal journey to discover one's true essence. Why not venture into the forest for a period, quite literally? Occasionally, a tree imparts knowledge that surpasses what can be gleaned from literature."

The following morning, one awakens gradually and perceives a profound tranquility within. You contemplate the serenity of the lake and reminisce about your younger self. You experience a profound state of serenity and calmness in the presence of your Inner Child. Your heart is filled with an abundance of love for your younger self. You reminisce upon the journey you embarked on in the mountains. You appreciate your resilience in surmounting obstacles, recognizing the inherent possibilities! You remain cognizant of the merits of detachment and expanded consciousness, refusing to succumb to your ego's desires and pluck the flower. You perceive no distinction between matters of great magnitude and matters of lesser significance. You are eager to proceed with your expedition. Upon awakening, you awaken and retrieve your Dream Journal to transcribe the details.

Lucid Dreaming Training

Mastering the art of lucid dreaming is facilitated when one possesses knowledge concerning the capabilities inherent in this state of consciousness. Familiarity with techniques to exert control over one's dream environment, sustain lucidity, manifest imaginary beings, and manipulate landscapes are pivotal factors that contribute to a heightened proficiency in lucid dreaming.

We shall conduct a thorough examination of each of these aspects.
Possible Activities in Lucid Dreaming

A fully realized lucid dream exhibits substantial tangibility and an abundance of intricate visual elements. The realm of dreams possesses boundless expansiveness, surpassing any concept you have contemplated of eternity. In the realm of lucid dreams, one is unencumbered by limitations or rules. The imaginings of your mind manifest themselves within your lucid dreams, leaving no bounds as to the possibilities that can be achieved within this state of consciousness.

One may choose to assume the persona of any iconic superhero from their childhood that they held in high regard, as depicted in films and interactive entertainment. You have the potential to assume the role of the remarkable Spiderman and rescue your preferred companion, Mary Jane Watson. One can travel from one city to another in a manner reminiscent of Iron Man, vigilantly observing the well-being of others. You have the option to engage in sexual relations with your most revered celebrity. One might have the ability to engage in temporal travel in order to partake in a forthcoming era whose appearance has long intrigued the vast majority of individuals.

One can employ cunning tactics and emerge victorious in every conflict, exhibiting the prowess of the most vigorous ninja. You have the opportunity to vividly recall and experience cherished moments from your childhood.

While these activities are enjoyable and entertaining, beyond the pursuit of mere illusions, there exists a plethora of possibilities to explore within the realm of lucid dreaming.

As per the insights of psychologists and dream experts, the phenomenon of lucid dreaming offers individuals the unique possibility to actively engage with the various facets of their subconscious mind through the act of interacting with the dream's characters. Additionally, it facilitates a more dynamic engagement with one's subconscious faculties through active participation within the dream state. Unveiling the state of lucidity will grant you access to a realm previously unimagined, bestowing upon you a profound revelation.

You possess the ability to exert control over the cosmos and influence the course of life events through the sheer power of your cognition.

How to Facilitate the Induction of Lucid Dreams

Remembering your dreams constitutes a significant stride towards generating lucid dreams with efficacy. It is imperative that one possess a deep acquaintanceship with their thoughts in order to discern the state of being in a dream.

"Here are a few suggestions that will assist you in cultivating lucid dreams:

1. Continuously inquire within yourself if you are envisioning the day, and engage in regular reality assessments at the utmost frequency feasible. By cultivating the practice of self-inquiry

regarding one's state of consciousness and diligently employing the aforementioned techniques for verifying the nature of reality, one shall be able to retain the ability to engage in the same consciousness assessment while immersed in the realm of dreams.

2. Consider attempting the practice of wake initiated lucid dreaming (WILD). The technique known as wake-initiated lucid dreaming involves the translation of one's wakeful state of awareness into the realm of dreaming. For this to be feasible, it is necessary to maintain a state of calmness and relaxation during the process of falling asleep. In order to attain the requisite state of tranquility required to transfer your conscious awareness into the realm of dreams, it is advisable to engage in a 10 to 15-minute meditation session prior to retiring for the night. Moreover, engaging in a mid-afternoon rest can offer similar benefits.

3. Enhance your familiarity with the signs that manifest in your dreams. This constitutes a significant factor that necessitates the practice of maintaining a dream journal. In order to familiarize yourself with the signs and symbols that correspond to your personal aspirations, encompassing visual and auditory elements frequently observed in your dreams, it is advisable to peruse the entries contained within your retrospective account of dreaming experiences. This will enable you to identify and acknowledge the presence of significant symbols, signs, and dream characters as they manifest themselves.

Prolonged Maintenance of Lucidity to Exercise Control over One's Dreams

Any factor that aids in maintaining clarity of mind bestows upon oneself the ability to exercise dominion over their thoughts. Presented herein are a number of easily implementable strategies aimed at sustaining and maximizing the transparency of your dream experiences, thereby enabling you to exert comprehensive mastery over lucid dreaming.

Use Lucidity-Enhancing Supplements

Throughout the course of history, the utilization of Galantamine as a cognitive enhancer has been an integral practice within Chinese culture for generations. The initial instance of employing this supplement derived from the Red Spider Lily for the purpose of augmenting mental clarity is attributed to the depiction by the venerable ancient Greek philosopher, Homer, who lauded its remarkable ability to heighten the intensity of one's dreams. Individuals who have experimented with this lucidity-enhancing medication attest that it is highly efficacious in stimulating and extending exceptionally vibrant, vibrant, and commonplace dream experiences. Research conducted on individuals who consume Galantamine indicates that this dietary supplement enhances the level of lucidity, intensity, precision, command, audacity, and duration of their dreams during sleep.

Nevertheless, it is crucial that you seek guidance from a healthcare professional regarding medical counsel.

Do Physical Activities

Participating in elementary physical exercises within the realm of your lucid dreams can effectively invigorate your cognizant mind, consequently extending the duration of your lucid dreaming experiences. Allow me to present certain instances of physical activities you may partake in to maintain transparency:

1. Engage in the motion of rubbing your palms together: This particular form of kinetic activity during the state of lucid dreaming fosters enhanced mindfulness of your dream physique and ensures that you maintain a sense of stability throughout the lucid dreaming experience.

2. Delicately patting oneself on the head: The act of delicately patting oneself on the head while lucid dreaming enables one to maintain an adequate level of consciousness, preventing any tendency for mental drift.

Summoning Dream Characters

The trajectory of your lucid dreams is determined by the presence of fantastical entities, underscoring the significance of acquiring adeptness in assembling the appropriate cast of dream personas.

Presented herein are a series of effective methods that are certain to facilitate your inquiry of renowned fictional characters from the realm of fantasy within the state of lucid dreaming:

✓ Request the Dream to Manifest a Specific Dream Character

The character of lucid dreams is such that it promptly accommodates your desires. Hence, any desire you may have within your lucid dreams promptly manifests itself. You may request the assistance of the expectation to provide you with a mentor for your dreams. After acquiring a dream guide, it becomes effortlessly feasible to solicit appearances of various fantastical entities resembling oneself two decades later, the most aesthetically appealing woman globally, one's ultimate inspiration, a legendary figure in cinema, beloved video game characters, and any other imaginative manifestations that one's yearnings may encompass.

✓ Observe Surroundings Anticipatingly

There is no requirement for you to engage in visualization exercises in this context. Merely observe your surroundings with the expectation of perceiving the desired dream figure positioned in the distance, patiently awaiting your command. It can be beneficial to confirm the presence of the individual you are seeking in close proximity. Occasionally, they may be lingering inconspicuously in the background, remaining unseen until verbally summoned. You have the option to verbally challenge them once you perceive their likely location, and await their emergence, or you may proactively seek them out.

✓ Discover the whereabouts of a Dream Portal.

All lucid dreams possess an infinite multitude of dream entrances. Locate a door and envision the desired dream character positioned directly behind said dream door.

Proceed towards the magnificent gateway of your aspirations, rotate the handle, and prepare to be astounded by the presence of the coveted individual poised gracefully beyond the threshold. Simply extend your hand towards the character, firmly grasp their hands, and draw them effortlessly into the realm of your vivid lucid dream.

✓ Mental Photoshopping

It is highly probable that your dream contains preexisting dream characters or objects. Employ the capabilities of your imaginative faculty to transform them into any preferred form or individual. Additionally, it proves beneficial to procure artistic tools with which one can paint or draw, create a preliminary illustration depicting the envisioned dream character, and then envision their manifestation emerging from the depths of darkness.

Modifying the Surroundings of Your Lucid Dream

Varied individuals who experience lucid dreams employ diverse techniques to alter the scenery within their dreams. Nevertheless, there exist fundamental methods that every novice lucid dreamer can employ in order to enhance the quality of their dream environment.

Listed below are the most effective methods for altering the scenery:

1. Rotate at a measured pace and contemplate the transformation of the scene: While engaging in rotational movement can be an advantageous method for exerting control over your lucid dreams, it is imperative to exercise caution and refrain from spinning excessively, as this may result in premature awakening. Executing deliberate and tranquil motions facilitates the alteration of the contextual landscape within your lucid dream. Envision the transformation of the scenery occurring as you rotate while keeping your eyes closed. Upon the completion of your spinning, the scenery shall bear resemblance to your envisioned outcome.

2. Kindly make a formal entreaty for a series of switches: Implore your mind's imagination to furnish a series of switches capable of regulating various phenomena, such as altering day to night

and vice versa, transitioning seasons from autumn to winter, activating past or future scenes, initiating the ambiance of a rainforest, waterfall, park, game reserve, and so forth. By manipulating these switches between their on and off positions while recognizing the outcomes they incite, you will witness the realization of your desired scenarios manifesting gradually with every switch flip.

3. Envision a fresh landscape as you traverse through the gateway of your dreams: Discover a door positioned within the heart of any of your dreamscapes and proceed to traverse it directly. Envision the desired scenery as you approach any metaphorical gateway to your aspirations. Upon entering through that doorway, it is certain that you will materialize exactly the scene that you envisaged.

4. Divert your gaze and visualize a fresh tableau unfolding amidst your surroundings: Cast aside the current scene you are witnessing, and conjure forth a completely different setting emerging in your wake. Envision the emergence of novel dream characters surpassing their existing counterparts. Upon your next encounter, you shall be astounded by the notable transformation in all aspects.

After examining the methods for proficiently mastering the practice of lucid dreaming, we will now explore advanced recommendations and strategies that can augment your level of lucidity, enabling you to fully relish the advantages of lucid dreaming.

A Study on Astral Projections within the Context of Lucid Dreams.

You may be familiar with the concept of astral projection, despite lacking an understanding of its essence and the methods through which it can be accomplished. Astral projection facilitates the alignment of your consciousness towards either the future or the past, granting you the freedom to engage in various activities without arousing notice.

During astral travels or projections, one can be considered to be in a state akin to being ethereal or immaterial. Your vivid dreams provide you with numerous chances to partake in these uncanny journeys to the astral realm. Astral journeys facilitate the exploration of realms beyond the confines of one's own consciousness, enabling individuals to engage with a vastly expansive celestial domain and thereby gain insight into events spanning the past, present, and future.

You can utilize specific sophisticated techniques for lucid dreaming to delve into the astral realm and extract greater value from your lucid dreams.

Presented here are several methodologies that can be employed to delve into the realm of the astral plane during the state of lucid dreaming:

1. To begin, initiate a state of lucid dreaming and augment your level of awareness by employing the methods that have previously been detailed for attaining these objectives.

2. Once you have entered a state of lucid dreaming, endeavor to return to the precise room where you initially fell into slumber preceding the translucent manifestation of your dream.

3. Carefully observe your inert physical form while you are in a state of slumber.

4. Perambulate the room and identify any item that has received minimal attention from you in the past.

5. Acquire the item, scrutinize it attentively and thoroughly, and allow the specifics of the object to be imprinted upon your subconscious awareness.

6. After rousing from slumber, retrieve the aforementioned item and ascertain whether the particulars documented within the realm of your vivid dream exhibit congruence with your conscious reality. If the particulars are in agreement, your astral projection will function optimally. In instances where there are certain inconsistencies, it indicates that certain manifestations of your thoughts were still present during your evaluation. It is necessary to engage in repetitions until one attains a flawless astral projection, unhampered

by the influence of the symbols and constructs within the mind.

7. Upon achieving profound success in astral projections, one gains the ability to traverse their domiciliary abode or local vicinity whilst engrossed in astral sojourns. Select a specific object or matter to scrutinize during these celestial explorations and conduct a verification procedure upon awakening to ascertain its precision.

Dream Yoga

This book originates from the practices of Indo-Tibetan Dream Yoga and draws inspiration from the rich heritage of the Tibetan Shamanistic Dream Tradition.

These customs were conventionally observed within the realm of lucid dreaming and necessitated the possession of skills in lucid dreaming.

Tarab Tulku derived the inherent universals and profound therapeutic techniques from these two traditions. He devised a system that is accessible for individuals of all backgrounds, requiring neither initiation nor a high level of attainment.

The system encompasses the pre-Buddhist tradition, commonly known as the Bon religion, shamanistic practices, as well as the belief system of Buddhism. The pre-Buddhist practice has a venerable history spanning several millennia. As an illustration, Tibetans held their dreams in high regard, and each morning, individuals shared the dreams they had experienced.

Dream yoga constitutes a segment of the Six Yogas, which encompasses a Tantric framework embedded within the context of Tibetan Buddhism. In this particular context, the term 'yoga' refers to meditation rather than physical exercises associated with yoga. Further insights into the Six Yogas will be provided at a later stage.

The Beloved Dream

Each of us has inevitably had aspirations that have had a significant impact.

What is the most remarkable dream you have had, a dream that has left a lasting impression and remains vivid in your memory?

Perchance, a reverie bestowed upon you fresh perspectives, aided in a momentous determination, or instilled joy and vitality within you.

Perhaps you encountered a long-standing acquaintance, a cherished individual, a creature of the natural world, or a potential romantic partner.

It is conceivable that you have conceived a significant scientific breakthrough within the realm of your dreaming.

It may encompass a vision from your early years or a more recent aspiration. It has the potential to cause a profound shift, evoke lightheartedness, amusement, or induce distress.

Let's find out.

The Dream You Loved

Your Imaginative Realm Serves as a Portal to Unleash Creativity

The contemporary rational culture imposes a sense of aridity and monotony upon our world, inundating it with an overwhelming presence of the conceptual mind. Our society is characterized by a fast-paced and demanding lifestyle, which tends to disconnect us from our innermost thoughts, resulting in heightened levels of stress, anxiety, and disturbances in sleep patterns.

Numerous individuals endeavor to alter this state by means of pharmaceuticals, alcohol consumption, substance abuse, adult material, indulging in excessive food consumption, or engaging in extravagant shopping activities. Regrettably, the situation continues to deteriorate.

Your imagined realm provides a gateway to endless creative possibilities and expansiveness of thought, bestowing upon you a sense of fulfillment, happiness, and delight. Moreover, the practice of lucid dreaming offers an innate euphoria, accompanied by a remarkable capacity to wholeheartedly relish one's existence.

Optimize your evening hours for maximum productivity.

Dreams and sleep present an exceptional avenue for engaging in profound psychological exploration and undergoing transformative experiences.

Lucid dreaming serves as a controlled environment for conducting research and analysis on the workings of the human mind. You are welcome to remain within the confines of the dream and thoroughly investigate its contents. One may conduct an exploration into the fundamental cognitive patterns that give rise to the manifestation of dreams.

Your subconscious mind possesses great power. Throughout the day, your conscious mind assimilates copious amounts of information, while during the night, your subconscious mind undergoes a period of nocturnal dormancy, wherein it meticulously analyzes and synthesizes the acquired data.

Your dreams possess an inherent autotherapeutic capacity, continuously operating to serve your well-being. Your subconscious mind inherently possesses the capacity to address your shortcomings and susceptibilities, effectively resolve challenges, and engender fresh concepts and innovations through the medium of your dreams. It is akin to possessing an internal counselor, scholar, innovator, and creative virtuoso.

Numerous artists and innovators have attained profound discernment and achieved crucial breakthroughs through the realm of dreams.

An example of this can be seen in the case of Paul McCartney, who crafted numerous songs while in a state of dreaming.

Moreover, dreams have precipitated noteworthy scientific breakthroughs. As an illustration, it can be observed that Elias Howe devised the sewing machine by virtue of a vision, which rendered to him the insight into the precise placement of the needle's aperture.

Furthermore, it was in a dream that Albert Einstein first discerned the principle of relativity. He envisaged himself gliding down a steep incline on a sled, progressively accelerating to the point of nearing the velocity of light. In that precise moment, the celestial bodies underwent a transformation in their visual manifestation, leading him to apprehend the fundamental principles underlying the theory of relativity.

The esteemed Finnish composer Jean Sibelius regarded dreams as a valuable wellspring of creativity and would inquire about his children's dreams each morning. In the event that one were to respond with "I am uncertain" or "I cannot recall," Sibelius inquired, "what sort of dream would you prefer to experience?"

Tarab Tulku and Manjushri are interconnected.

Tarab Tulku was an individual recognized as the eleventh embodiment of the revered Tarab Tulku lineage, embodying the profound spiritual legacy of Tibetan Buddhism.

He was discovered at the age of one. By the age of three, he had acquired the skills to comprehend written language and produce written material. Additionally, at the tender age of four, he assumed the responsibility of leading ceremonial observances.

He acquired the skill of dream practice during his formative years, and by the age of ten, his mentor organized a dream retreat exclusively tailored for young lamas. Initially, the instructor curated queries for the students, and prior to retiring for the night, they invoked the presence of Manjushri, a venerable bodhisattva renowned for wisdom, while reciting his sacred mantra. Subsequently, upon the manifestation of Manjushri in a dream, they proceeded to pose their inquiries, followed by a comprehensive deliberation on the responses during the ensuing morning.

It was discovered that Tarab Tulku possessed exceptional aptitude for lucid dreaming. In due course, news of this phenomenon disseminated, prompting a surge of individuals inquiring about various health and other predicaments, to whom he endeavored to provide solutions through his nocturnal revelations.

In the region of Tibet, individuals acquired the appropriate energy by engaging in meditative practices prior to entering the state of sleep. If individuals desired to harness the potency of sagacity, they engaged in the practice of meditation centered around Manjushri, whereas if their intention was to cultivate sentiments of benevolence and empathy, they directed their mental faculties towards the visualization of Avalokiteshvara.

You may also consider attempting it. As an illustration, in the case that you encounter difficulties in the realm of mathematics, it would be advisable to seek guidance from Einstein within the realm of your dreams. Similarly, if your aspiration is to pursue a career as a singer, it would be prudent to request private instruction from your esteemed idol.

Dream Incubation

Dream incubation serves as a means of acquiring knowledge and gaining insight within the realm of dreaming. It demonstrates optimal performance within the context of a lucid dream, although experimentation may be conducted with dreams in a non-lucid state as well. Your subconscious mind is capable of conceiving innovative solutions to difficult inquiries that may elude your conscious mind.

One can utilize the technique of dream incubation, for instance, to effectively resolve problems, cultivate new capabilities, seek guidance from a mentor, or engage in insightful conversations with a wise confidant.

The approach yields optimal results when you have dedicated considerable mental effort and extended periods of contemplation to the subject matter. Engage in contemplation of the problem prior to retiring for the night, endeavoring to condense it into a concise query or statement, such as...

What actions should I undertake in the foreseeable future?

I intend to engage in a lucid dream encounter with Albert Einstein, during which I shall pose inquiries pertaining to the theory of relativity.

Direct your attention to the subject you intend to explore prior to entering a state of slumber. Induce a state of relaxation in both your physical and mental faculties. Try not to think. Instead, employ your emotional intelligence and the power of visualization.

Please proceed as follows:

Please transcribe a problem in concise form onto a sheet of paper.

Memorize it.

Go to bed. Ensure that you have a writing instrument and notepad in close proximity.

Abstain from physical and mental tension. Release your cognitive understanding and utilize your emotional perception.

Reiterate the inquiry mentally and endeavor to form a mental depiction if feasible. Perform this action during the transitional state between wakefulness and slumber, known as the hypnagogic state. Persuade yourself to envision it during the process of falling asleep.

Upon awakening, it is advised to refrain from any physical movements. Please take note of whether you recollect any dreams and remain attuned to the associated emotions, allowing the dream to unfold.

Mentally recapitulate the dream.

In conclusion, kindly document this information.

Dream incubation is a time-consuming process that requires repetition in order to effectively operate. Therefore, exercise patience and allow ample time for the subconscious mind to process.

Additionally, it is advisable to refrain from employing dream incubation techniques for the treatment of profound emotional issues, as this approach could potentially induce feelings of anxiety or insomnia.

Nonetheless, should you perceive this approach as secure, you may discover intriguing concepts.

The Advantages Of Lucid Dreaming

Lucid dreaming entails a fully immersive encounter, as expounded upon in preceding chapters. It is an alternate reality in which one can reside unburdened by fears and limitations, with unwavering confidence in their capability to achieve anything they desire on a global scale. This newfound liberty vastly influences your conscious being. However, what impact does lucid dreaming have on the physical realm? Unquestionably, the peculiarity of an astounding Lucid dream diminishes over time - what then ensues? Herein lie several inherent benefits of lucid dreaming, encompassing both the state of slumber and wakefulness, providing tangible instances that will motivate you to enhance your realm of dreaming to a greater extent.

1. Lucid dreaming can facilitate the conquering of fears and phobias.

Do you possess a fear of heights? In the state of lucid dreaming, any apprehension will not hinder you from courageously parachuting out of an aircraft. Besides, the way that you will be protected, you can likewise hinder time and be in full control of your fall as you gently land on the ground. Numerous individuals who experience lucid dreams have attested to the profound sense of well-being derived from the ability to consciously manipulate their dreams, with some even managing to triumph over their real-life fears.

2. May assist in enhancing your ability to solve problems

This aspect of lucid dreaming is widely regarded as the most significant benefit by esteemed scientists and philosophers. They thought that it was one of the most noteworthy advantages since it is feasible for them to think about a specific issue when they dream. This procedure also fosters the establishment of neural connections within the brain, thereby generating diverse pathways and ideas to address imperative challenges or make critical decisions. It is also possible to employ lucid dreams for problem-solving purposes, whereby one can assess various solutions and examine their effectiveness within the dream.

3. Hone and enhance authentic aptitudes.

Would you be amenable to the notion that it is potentially feasible to engage in the application of your reality methodologies within the context of your lucid dreaming experiences, thereby enhancing the likelihood of success in your waking reality? This particular benefit stands out as one of the most remarkable and unexpected advantages of lucid dreaming. For instance, you can attend your driving lessons in reality and apply the concepts you have acquired during your lucid dreaming experiences.

In this way, you can ascertain how to accelerate your progress beyond what would have been achievable had you simply attempted it in conscious reality. It has the potential to facilitate cost and time savings, while simultaneously fostering your growth as a more skilled and proficient driver in a remarkably short period of time. One has the potential to engage in the practice of various life skills within the realm of lucid dreams, subsequently enhancing one's proficiency in said skills within the context of actual life.

4. Ceasing the occurrence of distressing dreams.

The overwhelming majority of individuals experience nightmares and recurrent dreams that involve distressing situations, such as falling off a frightful cliff or being pursued. Upon acquiring the skill of lucid dreaming, you will possess the ability to intervene in unfavorable dream occurrences, thereby granting you the opportunity to modify them and elicit positive outcomes. In the event that a presumed pursuit is transpiring, one may opt to halt their progress and confront any perceived obstacles, as this self-awareness will reveal the situation to be a product of one's imagination. Additionally, you will possess complete authority over the situation, enabling you to ensure your triumph in the conflict and bring an end to the distressing nightmare that plagues you.

5. Sexual Lucid dreams

One additional benefit of lucid dreaming is the opportunity for engaging in sexual experiences within the dream realm. This remarkable phenomenon allows individuals to manifest their desired partners, whether real or imaginary, effectively enhancing their dream state. You are able to engage in sexual activity as desired within a dream, and you have the freedom to choose any partner for such encounters. The inclusion of sexual experiences in lucid dreaming acts as a powerful catalyst due to the subconscious expectation that, in waking life, one typically maintains exclusivity with their chosen partner, if applicable. By employing this method, when you find yourself engaged in an intimate encounter with another individual, it will serve as an indicator that you are in a state of dreaming.

6. Healing of Emotional States through the Utilization of Lucid Dreams

Not all individuals are aware of the potential to leverage lucid dreaming for the purpose of emotional healing. The concept of emotional healing essentially refers to the ability to recover from psychological injuries. Feelings of deep distress, overwhelming anxiety, profound ambiguity, trepidation, and the enduring impact of distressing events are among the experiences that can be ameliorated through the practice of Lucid dreaming. The results can vary, differing from one individual to another. It is plausible that individuals who have experienced appalling circumstances could have a heavier workload, although it is also possible. If you happen to be contending with any form of illness, be it a chronic affliction or a minor discomfort, lucid dreaming is a tool worthy of consideration.

You have the option to seek consultation from an expert within your imagination or harness your inherent ability to consciously direct healing and recovery from within. The human psyche is regarded as a remarkable resource; contemplate the deceptive influence it possesses. For instance, if you find yourself perturbed due to certain circumstances, you may exert control over your imagination in order to articulate your concerns to your colleagues and supervisor. You will experience increasing levels of involvement and may stumble upon a solution that could potentially translate into your actual situation.

7. Lucid dreams can facilitate the revelation of your life's purpose." "Lucid dreams have the potential to aid in the exploration and realization of your true vocation." "The phenomenon of lucid dreams presents an opportunity for

individuals to uncover their true passion and ultimate life path.

An additional benefit of gradually increasing clarity in dream state lies in its potential to aid in the discovery of one's life's purpose. It is widely believed that life lacks inherent purpose unless individuals actively create their own. Through the practice of lucid dreaming, one can enhance the significance of their existence by cultivating conscious awareness. You may also revisit your motivation at a later time through the practice of lucid dreaming. Having clarity of mind enables you to examine the dream as it unfolds, rather than waiting until you are awake. This ongoing evaluation enables you to establish a connection and attend to your subconscious mind.

8. Enhance your capacity for creativity and innovation

In contrast to reality, your fantasies possess the ability to swiftly and immediately transform and materialize. With the flick of a wrist, one gains the power to eliminate, alter, and fabricate any object, allowing for swift mental engagement and the expeditious exploration of numerous possibilities. Paul McCartney, a member of the renowned band The Beatles, composed the entire melody for the popular acoustic track "Yesterday" within his imaginative realm. Similarly, Albert Einstein conceptualized traversing through a beam of light, which served as a catalyst for his groundbreaking theory of relativity. Niels Bohr, the founding figure of quantum mechanics, frequently referred to an inspiring vision that catalyzed his revelation of the molecular structure. Merely contemplate the potential cognitive processes that can be manifested by your brain during the state of lucid dreaming.

9. Deriving immense joy during the process of confronting the insurmountable

Lucid dreaming is arguably one of the most valuable experiences one could engage in. One may engage in any task without harboring any apprehension of self-harm or the possibility of committing an error. Through the practice of Lucid dreaming, one can extensively explore realms beyond imagination and awaken with profoundly pleasant memories of their dreams.

The tremendous stress experienced can become rather overwhelming at times, to the extent that it diminishes one's enjoyment significantly. Experiencing joy and engaging in activities that promote relaxation are essential elements for leading a contented existence. Following periods of strenuous activity, lucid dreaming can serve as a means of escape. Attaining an ample amount of enjoyment can be easily achieved without incurring any financial expenses. Additionally, it will not encroach upon your valuable waking hours.

During a Lucid dream, one has the ability to embark on a virtual journey across the United States in an imaginary automobile, partake in yachting adventures, navigate the slopes of the Swiss Alps for skiing, or showcase exceptional dancing skills amid the vibrant ambiance of a dance club. Please endeavor to initiate action and relax or enjoy yourself in your imagination, as it is indeed worthwhile to awaken feeling serene and content.

10. Experience comprehensive security

When one indulges in dreaming, they are creating their own ideal and distinct realm of imagination. You are capable of accomplishing all necessary tasks without arousing any attention. You have the ability to disregard the rules and standards of reality and establish your own set of regulations for asserting your claim. Embark upon the enigmatic and illicit.

11. Improve without risk or concern of harm or physical harm.

Professionals, scholars, and contestants proficient in the art of lucid dreaming employ their imaginative faculties to address challenges and acquire novel knowledge. Consequently, this advantageous aspect of lucid dreaming could yield a discernible enhancement in their interpersonal experiences. Consider the prospect of honing a specific skill, such as skateboarding, within an imaginative realm. You can practice it devoid of any hazards or anxieties pertaining to injuries. This particular cognitive activity has the capacity to propel you towards your ultimate objective in a similar vein, thereby augmenting your progress at a significantly accelerated pace.

12. Venturing into realms beyond the confines of the imagination

If one has ever experienced lucid dreaming, it becomes clear that lucid dreaming lacks a definitive set of instructions. Similar to the entirety of the cosmos, your fantasies possess immense potential and are incomprehensible in their profound connection with every sentiment in existence. When one experiences the phenomenon of lucid dreaming, one acquires the extraordinary ability to engage in activities that have hitherto remained beyond the realm of one's cognition. The realm of fantasy is enigmatic, harboring a multitude of enigmatic elements yet to be fully investigated. Embark on an exploration of this reality, thereby commencing the discovery of boundless potentials.

13. Acquire more TIME in your life

Collectively, we will spend approximately one-third of our lives in slumber. A THIRD. That represents a substantial duration, and you are, in any case, taking breaks throughout that period. Do you have any compelling rationale for lacking any inclination to experience bizarre phenomena in those imaginings? If you are indeed intending to be asleep during that period, it would be logical to acquire the skills necessary to MANAGE those dreams, correct? The prevailing benefit that Lucid dreaming offers. The greatest benefit arises from attaining the highest embodiment of oneself. You are directing your energy in a constructive manner, regardless of whether you are awake or in a state of slumber. You are effectively utilizing your time, and fulfilling the necessary responsibilities in your personal life. That merits any cost. I acknowledge that this may appear like an endeavor to promote a product; however, I must emphasize that these are unquestionably genuine benefits of Lucid dreaming, all of which have been proven effective. Lucid dreaming is an extraordinary skill that often goes unrecognized by many individuals. It is readily dismissed as being insincere or devoid of value. There exist numerous significant benefits and incentives to acquire knowledge, therefore, what is the reason for your hesitation? I have developed an introductory study guide designed specifically for beginners who wish to delve into all aspects of digital book creation. There is an abundance of knowledge to be acquired at the outset, and it is imperative to diligently engage in proper practice.

Prepare yourself for disconcerting occurrences as gossip may permeate everyday existence. Instances such as: facing public disgrace in the presence of your family, delivering a speech in front of external parties, engaging in a dispute or rivalry with another individual, possibly engaging in physical combat, attending a daunting job interview, and similar situations. Furthermore, notably, increasingly unconventional occurrences are likely to transpire should one embark on international journeys and engage in adventurous pursuits.

One can effectively prepare for such experiences through the practice of

Lucid dreaming, thereby mitigating their terrifying nature. Through practicing scenarios within a state of heightened self-awareness during a dream, one can effectively eradicate any lingering apprehension from one's consciousness. It relies on a highly systematic cognitive approach to alleviate fears, whereby one visualizes and gradually engages with them to foster adaptability. Through envisioning scenarios involving insects, such as dreaming, one can develop a diminished sense of fear towards them.

If you possess knowledge on the subject of lucid dreams, you will likely consider the phenomenon of sleep paralysis. The condition known as sleep paralysis of motion occurs when muscular functions are temporarily immobilized, signaling the body's readiness for sleep. Should you happen to regain consciousness during the course of this procedure, it can be a considerably disconcerting experience, as you may encounter symptoms such as paralysis.

Nevertheless, with the phenomenon known as lucid dreaming, this is not the case under any circumstances. Alternatively, it could be stated, "In addition, it is worth mentioning that one has the ability to exert greater REGULATION over this process, thereby effectively transforming it into a Lucid dream." If you happen to be an individual who encounters distressing sleep paralysis, Lucid dreaming can aid you in circumventing such experiences.

The History Of Lucid Dreaming

The historical origin of this specific dreaming phenomenon can be traced back over several years and possibly even to the Paleolithic Epoch. However, it was not until 1978 that lucid dreaming gained recognition within the scientific community. The initial verifiable records of lucid dreaming can be traced back to ancient civilizations in the East, dating back thousands of years.

Hinduism and Buddhism

There is ample evidence to suggest that lucid dreaming constituted a prevalent practice within the early Buddhist community, as indicated by various religious doctrines and teachings. The earliest documented account of lucid dreaming predates 1000 BCE and can be traced back to the Upanishads, which were transmitted through the ancient Hindu oral tradition encompassing spiritual teachings, philosophical insights, and wise sayings. The Vigyan Bhairav Tantra is an additional archaic

Hindu manuscript that elucidates the optimal methods for directing consciousness during the dream and visionary stages encompassed within the state of sleep. During the early centuries, the influence of India extended within the mountainous region of Tibet. For more than 12,000 years, the Bonpo spiritualistic tradition has upheld the incorporation of lucid dreaming within their meditative practices. Simultaneously, in the Eastern regions, Tibetan Buddhists held a prevailing belief that individuals could attain complete consciousness of their state of dreaming through the practice of dream Yoga, alongside the ancestral Indian tradition known as Yoga Nidra. The utilization of these Tibetan practices dates back to a period spanning more than 12,000 years.

The Tibetan Funerary text
The written heritage that has endured the amalgamation of this shamanistic tradition with Buddhism is the Tibetan Book of the Dead, which can be traced

back to the 8th century based on conservative estimates. Walter Y. performed a partial translation of this cryptic track in 1935. Evans-Wentz was the initial instance in which Western scholars, predominantly those studying history and esoteric knowledge, were introduced to these time-honored traditions. Subsequently, these time-honored customs had a profound impact on dream scholars during the 20th century, particularly within the realms of American psychology's Humanistic and Transpersonal schools.

The Ancient Greek civilization and the Islamic culture

The concept of lucid dreams is nearly as ancient as the origin of Western literature. Dreams held a position of prominence in the bedrock of Greek philosophy, as acknowledged by Aristotle. Plato and Socrates both directed their inquiries into the essence of existence towards our journeys in the dark of night. Aristotle initially expounded upon the notion of lucid dreams in his prominent work entitled

On Dreams, which was composed in 350BC. As per Aristotle, "during the state of slumber, there exists a faculty within our consciousness that informs us that the perception we encounter is merely a product of our dreaming state."
In the year 415 AD, there exists an additional historical account of the occurrence of lucid dreaming, as documented by the renowned theologian and philosopher, Saint Augustine of North Africa. He penned a narrative featuring a visionary character named Doctor Gratiae, wherein he made allusions to the concept of lucid dreaming, in what was described as one of his remarkable instances.
The role of lucid dreaming in the historical trajectory of Islam might have been pivotal. The Laylat al-Miraj experienced by Mohammed describes a nocturnal vision through which he gained a profound spiritual initiation. Ib El-Arabi, a renowned Spanish Sufi from the 12th century, postulated the notion that the mastery of mental faculties during the state of dreaming is an

indispensable skill for those embarking on the path of mysticism.

Centuries later, Sufi mystic Shamsoddin Lahiji meticulously documented a captivating celestial vision during the night, potentially indicative of a lucid dream encounter. As a result of the inherent cultural and historical disparities surrounding the differentiation between visions and dreams, discerning whether this narrative, as well as Mohammed's experience, took place during the state of sleep or in a visionary state, remains unattainable. Notwithstanding, it is unequivocally evident that they both exhibited clarity and mental alertness.

Regrettably, the practice of lucid dreaming was subject to suppression during the religious climate of Imperial Rome and the ascension of Christianity. Furthermore, numerous theologians held the belief that certain dreams possessed the capacity to unveil a deeper truth, while there existed a prevailing apprehension regarding the connection between witchcraft and dreams during this period.

Introducing Thomas Aquinas, an esteemed Italian theologian and philosopher. He exhibited great attention to detail in his convictions and aspired to reconcile Christianity with the philosophical perspective of Aristotle. Regrettably, this particular perspective neglected to account for the occurrence of spiritual phenomena through direct means. Consequently, he asserted that visions and dreams were derived from malevolent entities.

Following his admonitions, the collective Christian community began to question the reliability of dreams and visions, thereby giving rise to the prevailing practice of dismissing dreams that still endures in the Western world. Consequently, the practice of lucid dreaming became completely covert during the enlightenment era.

In the epoch of the Renaissance, the phenomenon of lucid dreaming experienced a resurgence as numerous individuals opted to relinquish their adherence to antiquated superstitions surrounding it and instead began to engage in introspection.

In addition, the esteemed philosopher Sir Thomas Browne also displayed a profound fascination towards the realm of dreaming. In his Religio Medici writings, he expounded upon his talent, stating, "...however, in a single reverie, I possess the capacity to create an entire comedic narrative, witnessing its unfolding, comprehending the witticisms, and awakening with amusement from the clever notions presented."

Furthermore, it was Rene Descartes who extensively expounded upon his dreams. Furthermore, he diligently maintained a personal journal wherein he meticulously documented numerous occurrences of his dreams. Regrettably, Descartes opted to maintain utmost confidentiality regarding his records on dreaming throughout his lifespan as a result of societal pressures exerted by the Church and scientific communities.

The initial acknowledgment of lucid dreaming in printed form occurred in 1867. Léon d'Hervey de Saint Denys authored a publication titled "Les rêves et les manières de les diriger ; Observations pratiques," which can be translated as "Dreams and the methods for controlling them; Practical Observations." He is widely recognized as the progenitor of lucid dreaming and was the first to introduce the term in his literary work. Nevertheless, upon its initial release to the general public, this literary work was disseminated without disclosing the author's identity. This publication presents a comprehensive analysis of Saint-Denys' dream journals along with an in-depth exploration of the phenomenon of lucid dreaming. Commencing at the age of 13, he commenced the practice of documenting the majority of his dreams, frequently discussing instances where the dreamer possesses a heightened sense of self-awareness within the dream state.

In a subsequent study conducted in 1913, the esteemed Dutch psychiatrist

Frederik van Eeden once again expounded upon the subject of lucid dreaming. In his literary work titled "A Study of Dreams," he conveyed, "Among the various categories of dreams, the one that piques the utmost curiosity and merits meticulous scrutiny is what I refer to as lucid dreams." During the period spanning from January 20, 1898, to December 26, 1912, I encountered and meticulously documented a total of 352 instances of this nature."

In 1968, an additional publication on Lucid Dreams was authored by the esteemed researcher, Celia Green. Green explores the profound disparity between lucid dreams and ordinary dreams. The researcher postulated that a correlation could potentially be established in the future between lucid dreaming and REM (rapid eye movement) sleep.

In the year 1975, the phenomenon of lucid dreaming was conclusively validated through a rigorous scientific investigation conducted within a laboratory setting. Psychologist Keith Hearne tactfully organized a session to document an occurrence involving Alan Worsley, an individual who possesses the ability to consciously control his dreams, within the premises of the esteemed University of Hull in England. Regrettably, this research failed to attain publication in widely recognized scientific journals. Stephen LaBerge had the privilege of being the first to publish data on the subject of lucid dreaming in 1978. The aforementioned data can be found in the publication titled "Exploring the World of Lucid Dreaming." Furthermore, he continues to be acknowledged as the foremost authority in the field of lucid dreaming research.

In the year 1980, researchers ultimately ascertained that the phenomenon of lucid dreaming is intricately linked to the rapid eye movement (REM) stage of sleep. Through the observation of individuals' eye movements while they were in a state of sleep, researchers were able to distinguish periods of lucid dreaming based on such eye movements. In the present day, researchers have the capability to augment an individual's capacity to experience lucid dreams.

Stephen Laberge further continued his noteworthy research on lucid dreaming, subsequently discovering that the cerebral hemisphere of the brain exhibited heightened activity during dream states when subjects engaged in singing. Conversely, the left hemisphere exhibited greater activity during the process of counting.

It is evident that the intrigue surrounding dreams dates back to ancient civilizations. A prevalent belief among individuals is that our dreams serve as vehicles for delivering meaningful messages. This topic attracts a significant amount of curiosity as it pertains to the frequent occurrence of dreams in the lives of a majority of individuals.

Experience the Unbounded Freedom of Lucid Aerial Exploration

When you embark on a flight, your level of consciousness becomes fully immersed in the entire travel ordeal. One may experience concerns about the possibility of falling (which may subsequently occur); however, by harboring unwavering confidence in one's capacity to soar, expressed through verbal affirmation of flight, one can ensure a triumphant journey in aviation. This one's a game-changer. The activity of flying with clarity is consistently reported as the most enjoyable pursuit among frequent dreamers.

Uncover novel realms and embark on temporal and spatial voyages.

Time travel dreams that are vivid and clear serve to eliminate the mental clutter. It is an opportune moment for meandering with a unique element. The realms of surrealism are intertwined throughout the past and future, prompting contemplation of whether one is traversing a fabricated temporal narrative or actually dwelling within an alternate dimension. The realm of lucid dreams encompasses numerous parallel realities. Every instance of waking within a different dream environment will present distinct phenomena and exceptional terrains to investigate. All of them exhibit utmost tangibility and an uncanny resemblance to real life. Similar to works within the science fiction genre, one has the ability to quantum-mechanically transport oneself to alternative realities, venture through divergent temporal pathways, embark upon extraterrestrial realms, and journey towards the hypothetical tenth dimension. The occurrence of a clear and vivid dream enhances the plausibility of virtually traversing alternate realms.

This captivating suggestion allows for the exploration of the essence of the physical cosmos as perceived by one's expansive subconscious. It is also possible to elicit an out-of-body experience (OBE) within a lucid dream, enabling one to explore the purported astral realm.

Partake in absolute seclusion.

In the state of lucid dreaming, individuals are able to conjure and immerse themselves within a personal and unique realm of fantasy. You have the ability to pursue all your ambitions discreetly, without anyone's knowledge. The conventional rules and norms governing real-world circumstances are nonexistent, allowing individuals to establish and enforce their unique set of rules. Thus, venture into the realm of the unseen and the forbidden. Ultimately, you are worthy and in need of this moment of self-sufficiency and lasting significance.

Generate Innovative Designs Ahead of Time

There exists boundless potential to preconceive and craft any conceivable utopian situation. Individuals adept in the art of lucid dreaming have the capacity to meticulously establish intricate narratives within their dreams, employing a skillful combination of dream-induced and wake-induced methodologies prior to entering the realm of slumber. The higher your level of enthusiasm towards the dream, the greater the likelihood of its manifestation. This has the potential to elicit lucid dreams by instigating prearranged narratives designed to serve as cues. Therefore, should you ever possess a longing to experience the sensation of cruising across the Mediterranean in a luxury yacht, or descending Mammoth Mountain on a snowboard, or soaring over the Grand Canyon on a hang-glider, you have the capability to do so.

.

Explore beyond imagination
If one has encountered the phenomenon of lucid dreaming, even on a single occasion, one would be aware that lucid dreaming lacks any definitive trajectory. Similar to the vastness of the cosmos, your dreams hold boundless potential and are incalculable in every aspect. In the state of lucid dreaming, one is

afforded the capacity to engage in activities previously uncharted by the mind.

Individuals proficient in the art of lucid dreaming are capable of engaging in personal encounters and interactions with their esteemed role models.

Numerous individuals who serve as personal role models instill in us the motivation to cultivate fresh perspectives and adopt novel approaches both in our personal lives and professional endeavors. Below are a few exemplary individuals who have greatly inspired me, including Wynton Marsalis. The Dalai Lama. Gavin Stephenson. Rick Braun. Warren Buffett. Elektra Moon. And we must not fail to acknowledge those who have passed, most notably Nikola Tesla. Neville Goddard. Bobby Hemmitt. Maya Angelou. Langston Hughes. Rev. Ike. Amelia Earhardt. Limits don't exist.

Whom would you elect to encounter in your state of lucidity? What inquiries would you pose to them? The possibilities are infinite, and these remarkable logical discussions can have a profound influence on your conscious existence.

Lucid dreamers have the capacity to alleviate grief by engaging in reunification experiences with departed individuals.

When we experience the passing of dear individuals, we obtain the perception that there are unresolved matters. Regardless of whether the demise occurs abruptly and without forewarning or gradually and foreseeably, we would all seize the chance to spend an additional hour with the departed. Lucid dreams involving deceased individuals may provide psychological therapy for the bereaved person. These manifestations offer solace and emotional restoration, even if one interprets them as psychological phenomena rather than actual visits from the departed. Lucid dreaming provides us with the necessary resolution to transcend our sorrow and progress forward in life.

Lucid Dreams

This location is where the enchantment transpires! For those who have derived pleasure from the process of recollecting their dreams, implementing reality checks, and embarking on aware dreams, the eventual experience of effortlessly attaining their first lucid dream awaits! Although the pace at which individuals encounter lucid dreams may vary, one commonality remains consistent for all. The remarkable encounters offered by their Lucid dreams are indelible in memory. An effective method to ascertain the occurrence of a Lucid dream is to assess if one can distinctly recall it with precision even after the lapse of several months. In the event that you do, it can be concluded that you experienced a Lucid dream. A typical dream tends to fade from memory quite rapidly. Frequently, lucid dreams tend to gain increased clarity with the passage of time.

One of my initial experiences of lucid dreaming in adulthood remains ingrained in my memory with exceptional clarity, notwithstanding the fact that it transpired over a decade ago. It commenced with me standing on a stage situated in the midst of an open expanse akin to the Texas landscape. Upon conducting a reality assessment, it proved unsuccessful, and subsequent to its failure, a sudden surge of liveliness permeated everything in a remarkably vivid manner. The gathering consisted of a limited number of spectators, and I found myself positioned on the stage. I was unsure of the purpose of my presence there, thus I glanced at the audience, and a bystander vocalized, "Are you not planning to commence the dance?" "That is the purpose for which we have all assembled!" Lacking alternative suggestions, I initiated a dance routine, eliciting applause for every gesture I executed. Subsequently, I performed an additional dance move, prompting a resounding applause from the audience, which added a humorous touch to the situation. Following this, I received a standing ovation after a few more dance moves. I descended the stage, at which point an individual approached me and exclaimed, 'Impressive performance!' I responded, 'Thank you for the kind words, although I must admit, my contribution was rather minimal.' In disbelief, he retorted, 'Are you joking?' That was great!". I was taken aback by the fervent acclaim my rather average dancing received from all present. A verdant meadow and an unpaved pathway were situated beyond the viewers. I desired to gain further knowledge in the domain, thus commencing my expedition on foot. A group of approximately eight individuals, whom I humorously referred to as my "fan club," began to trail behind me. The sun was radiating intense rays, prompting me to gaze directly at its light. I did not experience any discomfort in my eyes. It was the season of autumn, and the foliage displayed hues of orange and yellow. The radiant beams of the sun filtering through the foliage were truly awe-inspiring. The remarkable precision and vividness of the colors, the individual strands of grass, and every single element were of such extraordinary detail that it imbued reality with an ethereal quality reminiscent of a dream. I continued to stroll, experiencing an overwhelming sensation of affection within my being. In my vicinity, a group of laborers were diligently cultivating the soil using manual implements. It appeared as though they were engaged in the act of cultivating fresh produce. In the center of the field, a canine approaches me hastily. He displays immense joy upon my presence, as evidenced by the vigorous wagging of his tail and the display of his tongue. I approach him to interact with him and closely inspect his coat, and the remarkable precision of his hair is indescribably flawless. To the right, there stood a sizable crimson barn, and my innate sense suggested the presence of an aircraft within its walls. To express the extent of my exhilaration would be an understatement. I hastened my pace towards the barn, swiftly opening its doors and beholding a magnificent antique aircraft. I promptly entered the cockpit, whereupon I paused momentarily, appreciating the tactile sensation of the levers and the visual appeal of the dust settled on the glass. I remained astounded by the fact that this was merely a dream and that every aspect of my current experience was solely being generated by my psyche. I enthusiastically initiated the engine, sensing the palpable vibrations resonating throughout the vehicle as it sprung into action. I cautiously extracted the aircraft from the barn, brimming with anticipation over the prospect of taking flight amidst the vast expanse of the heavens. The expanse preceding the barn appeared to be of limited length; however, I noticed an unpaved thoroughfare to the right and deduced that in the event of insufficient velocity, the said pathway could serve as supplementary runway. I applied maximum power to the aircraft and, while accelerating rapidly, skillfully veered the plane onto the adjacent dirt road to extend the available runway. To my astonishment, an approaching blue truck was rapidly approaching. Attempting to maintain focus and disregard the presence of the truck, I endeavored to mentally override its presence. Subsequently, all facets of the dream began to dissipate, and I awakened in my place of repose. I have acquired a noteworthy insight from this Lucid dream experience, which is that any aspect brought into conscious awareness during a Lucid dream necessitates active interaction. Failing to do so may result in the disintegration of the dream itself. This has repeatedly transpired. In order for the Lucid dream to persist, it is imperative that we actively interact with any observed details or objects.

On occasion, due to underlying apprehensions, we inadvertently manifest scenarios in our dreams that can give rise to distressing encounters. It is essential to maintain cognizance of the fact that the individuals and situations we encounter within our dreams serve as manifestations of our inner thoughts and emotions. There is no cause for apprehension. In the event that a formidable warrior approaches you, wielding an axe, acknowledge their dedication and commendable commitment to physical fitness. Inquire with them regarding the most effective means of achieving physical fitness. Humor and commendation are the most effective mechanisms in combatting situations riddled with fear. In the realm of the subconscious, a modest allocation of effort in this vein will yield substantial consequences, given its high degree of responsiveness to thoughts. Through my personal explorations, I have come to the realization that demonstrating kindness towards all individuals inhabiting my dreams effectively eradicates any potential for unfavorable encounters. Ultimately, these entities are not inherently tangible or concrete, but rather subjective reflections of our individual ideals, emotions, and essentially synonymous with your own being. You should exhibit affection towards them regardless of circumstances.

In the forthcoming chapter, we will delve into the exploration of transcending constraints that impede our pursuit of even the most profound experiences.

Lucid Dream Summarized

- Lucid dreams encompass extraordinary, highly detailed encounters that are unlikely to be readily erased from memory.

- It is advisable to actively interact with any elements encountered during a Lucid dream, as failure to do so may result in the premature termination of the Lucid dream.

If you happen to come across any distressing experiences, employ the application of humor and commendation to redirect the dream towards a more positive trajectory.

- The encounter with a Lucid dream marks merely the initiation of a journey of exploration.

Collaborating With Your Spiritual Guides

Prior to delving into this topic, it is imperative for readers to possess a basic understanding of the notion of spirit guides and its original origins.

Although spirit guides are widely recognized in Western Spiritualist communities, their origins do not align with the contemporary concept of the "West." Spiritual guardians emerged within the African pre-colonial societies, encapsulating the profound spirituality that pervaded those civilizations.

Limited investigation has been undertaken regarding African pre-colonial spirituality; nevertheless, akin to a majority of indigenous spiritual traditions, there exists a profound focus on the influence of ancestral spirits in shaping the existence of the present generation. In contrast to the culturally appropriated concept of spirit guides prevalent in Western traditions, there is an absence of reliance on angels or archangels, which were introduced through Christianity, the prominent religious system of colonialism. The responsibility now rests squarely with the ancestors, who are often regarded as a form of the "undead" within the community of the living. Although it may appear reminiscent of a zombie apocalypse, the concept of deceased individuals coexisting with the living is entirely unrelated to such a scenario. Instead, spirit guides serve as dynamic entities, actively assisting and directing individuals they engage with in order to enhance their life circumstances through the applications of their profound ancestral knowledge.

In the year of 2016, the publication titled Ancestral Voices: Spirit is Eternal was authored by Dalian and Verona Spence-Adofo, presenting the outcomes of a comprehensive research endeavor spanning a period of seven years, dedicated to the exploration of African spirituality. Through their extensive research, they unveiled that African spirituality comprises six fundamental tenets, specifically:

- The concept of existence and its inherent characteristics

- Harmony and organization in existence

- The principle of interconnectedness and interdependence holds true.

- The social and spiritual hierarchy • The structure of spirituality and society • The order of spirit and societal systems • The ranking of spiritual and social entities

- The natural progression of existence • The rhythm of life • The sequential stages of being • The continuous pattern of existence • The perpetual cycle of living

- The essence inherently present in existence.

Everything that exists in African spirituality, whether it be living beings or inanimate objects, is regarded as encompassed within the Divine (panentheism - the belief that everything is within God). In African spirituality, there is an absence of canonical texts, as its teachings and beliefs are transmitted across generations through oral traditions, encompassing songs, spoken narratives, and wisdom teachings. This encompassing knowledge includes various aspects such as the utilization of medicinal plants for healing, spiritual healing practices, rites of passage, and communal customs.

The ethereal entities of African spirituality are purported to dwell within unseen abodes, engaging in communication with the living from a realm that coexists alongside the physical plane. In addition, it is widely believed among adherents of Judaism, Christianity, and Islam—representative of the three primary monotheistic religions—that actions occurring in the physical realm have a profound influence on the corresponding spiritual domain, and conversely.

Similar to other native belief systems, mankind engages with its surroundings in a mutually beneficial partnership that encompasses customs and heritage. The entirety of existence is acknowledged as encompassing those who have transcended to the realm beyond in the form of ancestral spirits. The predecessors are regarded as deities imbued with divine authority, albeit with a potentially less authoritarian connotation compared to how deities are conceptualized in Western societies.

Voodoo, characterized by its peculiar and sensational portrayal in Western society, encompasses a framework of ancestral deities that trace their origins back to pre-colonial African spiritual practices and their own system of spirit guides. In the practice of Voodoo, spirit guides fulfill a dual role by offering guidance to practitioners and intervening in human affairs upon being summoned by a particular community. The fusion of African spirituality and the colonialist Church in Africa resulted in a syncretic phenomenon where the saints of the Catholic Church were assimilated into the existing pantheon of ancestor-deities, commonly referred to as "loa." Over time, Voodoo came to be observed in colonies characterized by a substantial African population resulting from the transatlantic slave trade. The assimilation of the saints into the religious customs of enslaved Africans was a syncretic practice undertaken to appease the demands of slave owners, who insisted on the Christianization of their enslaved individuals. Consequently, a concealment was imposed upon traditional African spirituality, thus enabling its sustained observance in the colonies, specifically with a focus on Haiti, among other locations.

This concise and admittedly limited account of spirit guides is indispensable in achieving a more comprehensive comprehension as we engage in a discourse pertaining to their existence, their function, and their intended objective. We are about to approach consecrated ground, and I kindly request that readers proceed with utmost reverence in their approach.

Engaging with Your Spiritual Mentors

Should you have ever entreated St. Anthony for assistance in locating a misplaced item, such as your keys, you are well aware of the requisite course of action.

The ethereal guardians exist within the transcendental realm that lies beyond the confines of the material plane, and their eternal presence is perpetual. What they are not characterized by is autocracy. They demonstrate a high regard for your personal boundaries and will refrain from attending unless expressly invited.

However, it is important to note that spirit guides should not be equated to the religious figure of St. Anthony. Spirit guides do not serve as substitutes for the tooth fairy or the legendary "genie in a bottle." Their presence in the cosmos is not intended to place a coin beneath your pillow.

It is inappropriate to summon spirit guides for trivial matters. Their role is to provide guidance and support in your decision-making process. Please ensure that you maintain a sense of perspective when seeking guidance from the spirit guides, and kindly keep in mind the aforementioned advice by approaching this matter with utmost respect.

Spiritual guides would lack the capacity to offer guidance if they did not possess knowledge of at least one previous earthly existence. This reality offers a viewpoint regarding the physical realm, its obstacles, and its enjoyments. The non-corporeal entities, to put it differently, have not always existed in this manner. The indigenous paradigm of ancestral connection and communion involves the merging of the spiritual and material realms through the experience of incarnation. Additionally, it encompasses an inherent sense of ambiguity, particularly pertaining to the loa, within the practice of Voodoo. In our proprietary framework, which reflects the core principles of African spirituality, the consensus is that these two senses function in tandem. Our forebears are present alongside those individuals who uphold the identical fundamental ideals embodied by the loa of Voodoo, with the inclusion of numerous figures predating the era of colonialism.

In Catholicism, it is customary to offer prayers to the saints, whereas the loa play a role in serving the needs of the living. By fulfilling this role, they effectively serve as intermediaries between the Creator and all beings in both the spiritual and material domains.

Prior to delving into the exploration of your spirit guides (typically consisting of various entities forming a spiritual entourage), allow me to provide a comprehensive depiction of one of the pivotal loa in Haitian vodun, in order to establish a parallel with your individual spirit guides. (Note: Some of these may be known to you naturally, and at times, recollected from your past experiences or possibly discovered in old photographs.) However, visual identification of your spirit guides will not be possible. You will identify them through a significantly deeper bond.

Allow me to elucidate upon Erzulie Freda, a renowned loa who holds dominion over the realm of love. Freda belongs to the lineage of the Erzulie loa. This collection of loa is connected to the element of water, signifying qualities such as fluidity and the ability to undergo gradual transformations.

Freda, also referred to as "Lady Erzulie," is renowned for her coquettish nature, consistently leaving her admirers dissatisfied, and engaging in the act of "riding" individuals during spiritual possessions in a trance-like state. Freda also maintains a connection with Our Lady of Sorrows, a venerated figure within the Catholic Church, thereby demonstrating the presence of syncretic elements in her worship. Our Lady of Sorrows is a revered saint within the Church, symbolizing the role of Mary as the anguish-filled mother of the Crucified Christ. Therefore, Erzulie Freda encompasses traits beyond that of a persistent seductress and capricious romantic partner. Additionally, she is the mother who endures affliction.

The intricate nature of this deity exemplifies the extent to which the Voudon loa system surpasses the recognition it receives from public perception. A similar assertion can be made regarding the role of spirit guides within the Western paradigm and the endeavor to achieve lucid dreaming - it is indeed a complex matter.

Hence, I desired to offer a contextual framework pertaining to the manner in which spiritualism in the Western world has sought resolution for its evident spiritual unease by incorporating elements from diverse cultural actualities. Due to the historical foundations underlying the belief in spirit guides, which date back to prehistoric times, comprehending these intricacies holds greater significance than one might initially perceive.

The reality is that when delving into the realm of spirit guides and attempting to determine your own, you are establishing a connection with a venerable human tradition that has endured for innumerable generations. Widespread among all native populations prior to the intrusion of colonialism, it is worth noting that we all had indigenous origins at some juncture in history. Hence, these customs and practices can be considered as a testament to human heritage. However, the European West has chosen alternative spiritual frameworks to replace those of the ancients, resulting in a disconnection from the significance of these ancient cultural remnants which serve as a crucial part of our human heritage. In this sacred moment, we are re-establishing our connection to the timeless source of spiritual nourishment - our progenitors and the ethereal beings of profound knowledge.

Connecting

You have consistently had the presence and guidance of your spiritual companions. They have consistently possessed knowledge of and displayed concern for your well-being.

These ethereal beings have previously undergone the human existence. They are regarded as your forebears, albeit potentially for a fleeting period, given that spirit guides are undying entities traversing numerous terrestrial manifestations.

When engaged in introspection or contemplating difficulties or obstacles, we draw upon the valuable insights gleaned from past experiences. We recollect the counsel bestowed upon us by individuals of great wisdom in our vicinity. We revert our attention back to the instructional content. This introspective discourse with historical events and experiences constitutes an integral facet of the spirit guide's essence. They possess not only an intimate understanding of your persona, but also an extensive familiarity with the intricacies of the world, albeit in a significantly more profound and comprehensive manner.

We perceive the internalized reflections of individuals who provided guidance during moments of adversity in our existence. We seek their advice. We engage in the same practice with the assistance of spiritual guides. At times, it is the spiritual mentors who proactively extend their guidance to us along our life journeys.

I have experienced this occurrence twice. Regarding the initial instance, I was in an adolescent stage. Being the elder of my two siblings, I was given the privilege of having the secluded quarters of a spacious, lower-level chamber. During one evening, I became conscious (although I now realize it was likely a state of lucid dreaming). I observed a lady positioned at the threshold of my chamber, donning a summer garment adorned with intricately patterned blossoms, a hat made of straw, and spectacles shielding her eyes.

Without delay, I swiftly positioned my head beneath the covers and commenced emitting distress signals for the attention of my parents. I was completely unaware of the identity of this enigmatic woman and the reasons behind her presence at the entrance to my room. She was the initial visit I had the opportunity to encounter.

The second visit that I am able to distinctly recollect is a dream that I experienced during my adulthood. This dream did not exhibit the characteristics of lucidity, but instead was a typical, non-lucid dream. I found myself positioned alongside the street during the nighttime hours, with the steady stream of vehicles passing by. Abruptly, a Citroen automobile swiftly traversed the vicinity, brimming with a multitude of female passengers. All the women appeared to be of mature age and had their heads adorned with kerchiefs, from which long braids gracefully fell. As they proceeded, they summoned my attention and gestured cordially. They were exhibiting a plethora of gold teeth while wearing joyful expressions on their faces. Upon awakening, I became cognizant of the fact that I had encountered my spiritual guides.

I exclusively encountered these unplanned visitations. Upon developing my comprehension of spirit guides and their purpose in guiding me towards my path in life, I initiated regular communication with them. As an author, I frequently engage in introspective dialogue (a common aspect of the craft), although I am cognizant that I am not truly conversing with myself. The thoughts that were previously held within are now expressed outwardly, resulting in a dialogue that exists within both current and past time periods. Through the guidance of spiritual mentors, we are granted access to profound wisdom and knowledge that surpasses that which was obtained through previous interactions with learned individuals. The extent and range of information that can be imparted to us is significantly enhanced.

The occurrence of spirit guides engaging in direct "outreach" is more prevalent than one might perceive. If one is not accustomed to their presence, such as myself during the encounter with the woman in the fashionable summer attire, it is possible to overlook indicators of attempted communication. There are several significant indications that this is the case.

- Heightened occurrence of extremely vivid lucid dreams, often involving visitations. These dreams may potentially encompass visual representations of your guides, as I have personally encountered on two occasions.

• Encounter with emblematic objects - such as white feathers manifesting in your vicinity or upon your person, discovering misplaced keys in extraordinary or unforeseen locations, and the unexpected appearance of other peculiar articles, a few of which may possess distinctive relevance to you.

• Intuition is refined. • Intuition becomes more acute. • Intuition is enhanced. • Intuition is heightened. We expeditiously and assuredly form conclusions regarding situations and individuals.

• It is possible that you will have a novel response to music, as if you haven't experienced it in the past. If that is the case, promptly search for the lyrics online in order to ascertain if they may potentially provide insights or resolutions to the inquiries currently occupying your thoughts.

• Consistently encountering a word, a phrase, or a number on multiple occasions. This is an indirect endeavor to address the initial inquiry through alternative methods.

• The abrupt sense of urgency to undertake an action or visit a place that had previously been regarded with little significance. One might experience an inclination to proceed without a thorough grasp of the underlying rationale. Devote some time to the experience in order to evaluate it. If this issue continues, you will be contacted

Inviting

Spirit guides only intervene in the affairs of their charges when visitation has become an urgent necessity in their wise opinion. During my inaugural visit, I was traversing a challenging phase of childhood known as pre-adolescence. Despite providing reassurance, my guide inadvertently instilled fear within me.

Until now, I cannot ascertain the exact reason, though I hold the belief that it pertained to the significance the transition held for a young woman. It is plausible that she had perceived it as an imperative necessity, as I was not adequately prepared for the subsequent events that unfolded upon the arrival of the day.

Frightening! I apologize for my outburst, esteemed summer spirit guide. I was in dire need of your guidance, even though I was not aware of it. That is the crucial point to bear in mind regarding the function of spirit guides. They function as an inherent aspect that lies beyond your grasp. It represents the existing reservoir of knowledge within you that you consciously choose to ignore or disregard. They bring it to light, allowing you to utilize it as a vital life skill.

During the second occurrence, I found myself in a period of my life where I had developed acquaintanceship with a family whose underlying dysfunctionality had previously eluded my awareness. At that time, I perceived the father as being unconventional, yet also possessing autocratic tendencies and a disposition for control. I began to perceive the man's idiosyncrasies as indicative of an underlying disturbance within him. It was sinister.

The situation escalated to a point where the man's spouse, relative, and the elderly cohabitant met their demise at his hands. My guides had arrived to forewarn me. The vehicle in which they were traveling happened to be identical to the one driven by the abusive spouse, including sharing the exact same hue. I will refrain from providing the distressing particulars of the situation, but I am grateful for having survived that ordeal, and I express my gratitude towards my spirit guides, who don gold tooth prosthetics and traditional babushka headscarves.

Hence, one can infer that circumstances must be exceedingly challenging for them to seek your assistance. Initiating outreach efforts demonstrates a proactive approach towards fostering a mutually beneficial relationship that can yield greater advantages for both parties involved. Your outreach isn't something that happens every day in the world of the spirits – where far too many languished unfulfilled due to the contemporary West's spiritual malaise.

The act of summoning your spirit guides is akin to engaging in various forms of prayer, affirmation, or mantra. The invitation serves as a strong indication to your spiritual guides that their purpose is duly acknowledged. Not only does this provide them with a sense of comfort, but also adds to their committed spiritual exploration in their state of disembodiment.

The establishment of a fruitful and courteous rapport with a spiritual guide can only arise from the identical foundation of friendship: Authentic empathy, authentic shared interest, and a firm commitment to authenticity. Engaging in insincere tactics will not yield any favorable outcomes when dealing with the refined spiritual mentor. They possess knowledge about the hue of bovine excrements.

Select Your Framework Based On Your Conviction

I trust that you are becoming enthused about the prospect of exploring spirit guides from a renewed perspective. In addition to this, I would like to invite readers to contemplate the notion that possessing a resolute assurance regarding the paradigm through which they engage with their spirit guides is the sole determinant of its efficacy.

You are obligated to have faith in what you are endeavoring to accomplish. Hence, if one is unwilling to embrace the notion of an ethereal realm that exists in tandem with our own, what does it truly matter? In my perspective, prioritizing the endeavor to establish a connection with an aspect of oneself that can solely be unveiled by them supersedes that consideration.

If it provides you with a sense of ease, you may categorize them as psychobiological functions. The concept of lucid dreaming or the aspirations of encountering spirit guides do not pertain to subscribing to any particular ideology. In truth, ideology presents itself as a foe to rationality, demanding the relinquishment of discerning thinking in favor of dogmatic beliefs or personal revelations.

You possess autonomy over your thoughts, and it is solely your responsibility to determine their application, within reasonable limits.

Therefore, whether originating from our evolutionary history or existing as ethereal beings, spirit guides are readily accessible to you. They possess knowledge that eludes you and take charge of paths you have yet to traverse.

Indeed, the exploration of the subconscious necessitates the presence of a competent and knowledgeable guide. Exercise your discretion and receive a gratifying experience, one that will enhance your life and bring about profound transformation.

The Roles And Significance Of Lucid Dreaming

There is an illuminating aspect amidst the obscurity conveyed by the statement "the significance of lucid dreaming is not surpassing that of ordinary dreaming." By referring to "the function," I intended to imply that lucid dreaming possesses a degree of usefulness. It serves a purpose by providing clarification to individuals seeking understanding regarding the necessity of such dreaming experiences. I have condensed it to save your valuable time.

Mind Control

Regrettably, that is not my intention - I do not imply that you possess the ability to manipulate the thoughts of others. What I am trying to convey is this. By engaging in the practice of lucid dreaming, individuals will enhance their capacity to effectively regulate their mental faculties.

As you can find later, practicing lucid dreaming requires your efforts to control your mind. The mind is inherently challenging to regulate, and achieving complete mastery over it can be regarded as an exceedingly formidable task. The concept of mind control denotes liberating ourselves from the dominion of the mind.

When operating within the confines of our cognitive faculties (or being cognitively identified), we have a propensity to swiftly transition from one train of thought to another. Being mindful in this particular state proves to be highly challenging, despite the fact that mindfulness plays a pivotal role in achieving successful lucid dreaming. How can one have awareness of being in a state of dreaming if they lack mindfulness? That is the point. Upon embarking on the journey of developing this skill, it is imperative that you cultivate a state of mindfulness. Mindfulness is a prerequisite for all forms of psychic and spiritual practices.

Mindfulness cultivates heightened self-awareness and offers boundless benefits in everyday existence. Mindfulness holds significance not just in the realm of dreams, but also within one's waking existence. This function presents an unprecedented opportunity to experience the utmost advantages derived from the practice of lucid dreaming.

Self-Exploration

No doubt. By means of engaging in lucid dreaming, one is granted the opportunity to embark upon an exploration of the boundless realm within oneself. Given that dreams serve as the psychological expression of our subconscious wishes or desires, whether knowingly or unknowingly repressed within our unconscious mind, it follows that lucid dreaming can be regarded as a means of self-exploration.

Every individual has the capability to undergo the phenomenon of lucid dreaming, however, each person's experience is distinctive. The subjective phenomenon encountered during lucid dreaming is inherently distinctive and defies direct comparison to the lucid dreaming experiences of others. The perception of undergoing such an out-of-body encounter may be similar from person to person, yet the actual experience cannot be identical.

This earth is ours. We share things. Nevertheless, the subconscious mind belongs to you. It is your world. In that location lies your database, which governs the majority (95%) of your daily existence. Engaging in the exploration of this "realm" entails delving into the depths of one's own being. The act of engaging in lucid dreaming does not result in a deeper comprehension of the practice itself, but rather leads to a heightened self-awareness.

Higher State of Awareness

The acquisition of additional information regarding dimensions that extend beyond this physical realm leads to the achievement of an elevated level of consciousness.

Through the attainment of lucid dreams, individuals gain a heightened consciousness regarding the existence of dimensions that extend beyond the confines of the physical realm. Your subconscious mind serves as a realm, an intricate storage facility where your abilities are stored or repressed. Primarily, we engage in a routine resembling that of automatons. We persist in adhering to our daily routines and familiar circumstances, resulting in a loss of purpose or orientation over time. A high-end characteristic of embodying a mechanized existence resides in the absence of self-awareness.

By elevating our self-awareness to a heightened level, we gain a greater consciousness of our own being.

As a result, the enhancement of our quality of life becomes significantly attainable. We can assert authority over ourselves, our desires, our actions, and the like. Furthermore, it is widely acknowledged that achieving an elevated level of consciousness enhances individuals' wisdom. When we refer to "wiser," we are implying the ability to cease engaging in unfavorable choices.

Overcoming the Limiting Beliefs

Limiting beliefs act as obstacles to the realization of dreams and aspirations. They stiflle your creativity, undermine your drive, and diminish your aspiration for self-improvement. Limiting beliefs pertain to notions that one holds about their inability, unfortunate circumstances, insignificance, lack of uniqueness, and the perception that certain objectives or tasks are deemed impossible, among others.

These are the convictions that constrain your ability to realize the full range of opportunities in your life. They impose constraints that hinder one from attaining greater heights and positions of higher significance. Overcoming these convictions while conscious presents a challenge. Overcoming these challenges is more feasible within the realm of lucid dreaming.

It has been conveyed to you that the phenomenon of lucid dreaming possesses a certain degree of controllability. Given that lucid dreaming is a neurological phenomenon, the ability to exert control over the lucid dreaming experience can be attributed to the regulation of said neurological processes. Look. The acquisition of a novel language induces alterations in the neural connections within your brain. New neural connections are formed whenever new knowledge is acquired.

The alteration of habits further leads to the modification of synaptic patterns within one's brain. From this perspective, should you make a decision while in a state of lucid dreaming, no matter how insignificant the alteration may appear, it will undeniably materialize.

The constricting notions or inflexible mentality can be attributed solely to the neural connections within the brain. One can alter their mindset or transcend their limiting beliefs by engaging in the practice of lucid dreaming.

Are you familiar with any information regarding hypnotherapy? I bet you do. In the practice of hypnotherapy, the therapist facilitated the client's entrance into the depths of their subconscious mind. The hypnotherapist facilitated his visualization of engaging in a swimming activity. The client exhibited an intense fear or aversion towards this. The task proved challenging for the client, as they encountered difficulty in both swimming within the hypnotic state and within their vivid imagination. Eventually, he made it. The cessation of distress caused by this specific phobia occurs. The level of clarity in the hypnotic imagination may be comparatively lower than that of lucid dreaming, yet it presents an opportunity for a transformative shift in one's mindset. Lucid dreaming is considerably superior in comparison.

Finding the Answer

At a certain point in time, you found yourself grappling with a dilemma. You communicated to your acquaintance that you are expecting to receive some information from her. Following her statement, she inquired, "Contemplate the matter, if you will. How could this occur?"

Spiritualists hold the perspective that the authentic Guru resides within the depths of our own being. Contemporary society holds the belief that genuine knowledge is acquired through direct personal encounters. In contemporary society, it is referred to as the elevated essence of one's being. Irrespective of the terminology one prefers, it is imperative to acknowledge the necessity of this particular requirement. It is not in reference to your heart. It pertains to the embodiment of your higher intellect, heightened awareness, and authentic self.

According to certain ancient customs observed in East Indonesia, encountering oneself within a dream can be indicative of an imminent mortality. It is widely acknowledged that your higher consciousness has emerged in order to notify you of your imminent departure from this corporeal vessel. It is time to bid you farewell. Indeed, the matter at hand is quite perplexing, wouldn't you agree? It signifies the act of bidding farewell to one's ego, encompassing the physical, intellectual, and emotional aspects.

In the realm of lucid dreaming, one has the capacity to encounter "said individual" in order to obtain a resolution to a predicament. Naturally, the inquiry should pertain to your personal experiences. Take marriage, for instance, during a certain phase of your life, you may be uncertain about the course of action to take. One may engage with their inner spiritual guide or seek guidance from an enlightened being residing within oneself to assist in reaching a resolution. At times, the reflection in the mirror may resemble you, while on other occasions, it may present an improved likeness.

The Gateway to Enhancing Other Psychic Abilities.

I hold the conjecture that individuals who engage in reading material regarding lucid dreaming are also inclined towards perusing content on other psychic abilities such as astral projection, remote viewing, psychokinesis, clairvoyance, and similar phenomena. In any case, they are perusing a portion of them.

Should you ascertain or concur with this supposition, then it follows that you readily acknowledge this to be the foremost advantage that lucid dreaming can provide. Yes. Lucid dreaming serves as a gateway to the cultivation and enhancement of other parapsychological abilities.

In order to partake in the phenomenon of lucid dreaming, it is necessary to stimulate and engage one's more delicate sensory apparatus. Lucid dreamers, when perceiving and interacting with their dream environments, employ their more delicate faculties. In the realm of dreams, the faculty responsible for perception is not attributed to our physical eyes, but rather the ethereal organ commonly referred to as the third eye or the inner eye of the mind.

The corporeal form is not our sole embodiment. We possess more refined corporeal forms, including the cognitive entity, energetic entity, ethereal entity, astral entity, and others. These entities are constantly engaged in their functions, yet our attention seldom dwells upon them. The inherent predisposition of our cognitive processes is directed towards the physical form.

These entities are operating as the means of transportation. We, as sentient beings, operate and control these vehicles. Nevertheless, it is not feasible to operate these vehicles concurrently. While operating a given vehicle, the remaining vehicles operate autonomously in accordance with the directives generated by the subconscious.

When the pursuit of psychic exploration is desired, we opt for an alternate means of conveyance. An instance of this is when one engages in energy healing, whereby they harness and manipulate their pranic body. In the context of astral projection, the utilization of one's astral body is imperative. These entities serve as the conduits through which you embark upon the exploration of various metaphysical realms. The manner in which one operates these vehicles is through active engagement and a constant awareness of one's presence within them.

I previously mentioned that lucid dreaming serves as a gateway to other avenues of psychic development due to the ability to redirect one's consciousness from the physical body to more ethereal aspects of being. In these more refined corporeal forms, the more refined receptors are positioned. Hence, the act of engaging in lucid dreaming will facilitate the mastery of other psychic disciplines. Furthermore, the acquisition of the skill of lucid dreaming serves as the most accessible gateway to mastering other levels of psychokinesis.

Many novice individuals often find themselves transitioning into the practices of remote viewing or astral projection while experiencing lucid dreams. This phenomenon can occur as individuals acquire the ability to regulate their more refined corporeal forms. Seasoned individuals who possess adeptness in lucid dreaming have the ability to consciously initiate astral projection within the realm of lucid dreams.

During one of the days in my training, I emerged from my slumber. Nevertheless, I possessed the ability to perceive things lucidly in the realm of my imagination. I sensed the presence of the pillows, however, my vision transported me to an alternate location that was not a deliberate creation of my imagination. Subsequently, I ascertained that it pertained to the practice of remote viewing.

Numerous authors incorporate the concept of "divergence" into the implementation of lucid dreaming. I strongly differ with this viewpoint as segregation is solely necessary in the practice of astral projection. Astral projection and lucid dreaming are distinct modalities of the psychic realm. We have engaged in a discussion regarding the nature of the dream. Astral projection does not correspond to a mere dream state. The investigation involves the examination of various planes of existence wherein reside alternate forms of living entities. There exists a potential peril associated with astral projection, specifically, the unlocked astral portal may be susceptible to intrusion by astral entities. The occurrence of lucid dreaming is devoid of any association with this particular risk. Hence, I hold a divergent viewpoint regarding the notion of "separation" in lucid dreaming, as its implementation appears futile.

May I inquire as to the mode of transportation utilized within the realm of lucid dreaming? It represents the cognitive aspect of an individual. When I say "mental," I am not referring to the sensation. I am referring to cognitive intelligence, encompassing components such as imaginative faculties, the ability to visualize, employ auto-suggestion, and other pertinent cognitive abilities that will be examined throughout the various sections.

What is the sensation like?

Lucid dreaming retains the fundamental essence of dream-like qualities, rendering it indistinguishable from conventional dreaming experiences. Nevertheless, it is a vision characterized by an elevated state of consciousness. It is possible for one to recall one of their dreams. You have the ability to recollect the events or visuals that transpired. One is unable to recollect the sensation experienced upon touching, hearing, or smelling stimuli within a typical dream. Furthermore, your options are limited to mere observation.

Envision a scenario wherein your recollected dream exhibits enhanced clarity on multiple occasions; wherein you are able to perceive sensations, auditory cues, and olfactory stimuli, and wherein you possess a certain degree of control over its unfolding (although complete control over all aspects of lucid dreaming remains elusive, analogous to a sailor having limited control over the vast ocean). This is the manner in which the experience of lucid dreaming manifests itself. Nevertheless, such information alone will provide little insight, as personal experience is imperative in gaining a true understanding.

Lucid Dreams
The ultimate classification of dreams pertains to lucid dreaming, which van Eeden deems the most captivating among all dream experiences. When engaging in lucid dreaming, an individual achieves a state of heightened consciousness, wherein they possess impeccable awareness and possess the

ability to exercise volitional control over their focus. The uninterrupted state of sleep during the phenomenon of lucid dreaming results in an individual feeling revitalized and stimulated in terms of their cognitive processes, particularly in the realms of creativity and analytical problem-solving. Van Eeden held the viewpoint that the meticulous examination of lucid dreams is warranted due to their intricate nature and intriguing attributes.

The concept of lucid dreaming may appear unfamiliar and pose a challenge to comprehend for those who have not previously encountered it. However, you can gain a grasp of the lucid dreaming phenomenon by drawing parallels to the more acquainted state of consciousness you currently possess. The crux of the matter lies in fostering consciousness.

Become Aware

One of the simplest methods to initiate awareness is by engaging in a mindfulness exercise. Practicing mindfulness entails residing in the present moment and possessing a heightened consciousness of the events unfolding during that precise juncture. The cognitive state that individuals experience during the practice of mindfulness bears resemblance to meditation, wherein one attains a heightened level of consciousness and becomes cognizant or lucid within the present moment. It constitutes a notable parallel to the potential encounters one might encounter throughout the state of lucid dreaming. Engage in the subsequent brief exercises for a comparable effect akin to that of lucid dreaming.

Awareness in 5-4-3-2-1

Gaining consciousness of your senses constitutes an integral aspect of meditation and employs the principles of mindfulness to fully live and embrace your present circumstances. This exercise presents itself as an exceptional choice for individuals facing the challenge of overwhelming emotions, particularly during moments characterized by panic attacks, as it effectively aids in directing and centering the mind.

Exercise vigilance and adhere to the following instructions:

Utilize your vision to identify five observable objects in your immediate surroundings. Please verbalize the objects you are perceiving internally or externally and allocate sufficient time to fully observe each item before transitioning to the subsequent object.

Enumerate four sensory perceptions that can be experienced internally. Articulate the sensation either verbally or internally, and engage in deep inhalations while undergoing the sensation.

Perceive three auditory cues and subsequently identify them either in your thoughts or by vocalizing them. Take a moment to actively listen to each individual while engaging in deep and controlled breathing.

Please identify and silently or audibly name two olfactory sensations in your immediate surroundings. Inhale the scents fully.

Finally, ascertain one flavor, or in the event that you are unable to perceive taste, consider a preferred flavor. Please pause for a moment to reflect on the flavor.

As an illustration, while located in one's sleeping quarters, various outcomes may be observed as a result of engaging in this exercise.

- There are five visual elements present: the exterior garden, neatly placed towels on the bed, a canine companion, a wardrobe in the room, and curtains that adorn the windows.
- I am able to perceive four sensations: the rhythmic expansion and contraction of my chest with each breath, a gentle tingling in my fingertips, the warm exhalations of my canine companion against my leg, and the refreshing touch of cool air on my skin, courtesy of the fan.
- There are three auditory elements present: the melodious chirping of a bird outside, the audible presence of music playing, and the tranquil sound of the water fountain in the yard.

- The presence of two fragrances can be detected: the aroma of freshly brewed coffee and the scent of newly mown grass.
- A single sip: the fragrant essence of coffee lingers in my breath.

Develop an understanding of the respiratory mechanism.

This subsequent exercise is centered around cultivating mindfulness of your breath. Have you given consideration to your respiratory pattern thus far? Frequently, we remain unaware of our constant breathing, despite the fact that it is an innate activity that we engage in continuously throughout each day. Please pay attention to your current breathing pattern. Does it have a high or low rate of speed? Are you inhaling deeply or taking shallow inhalations?

Please retain your breath momentarily, and subsequently release it in a gradual and controlled manner. Take a deep breath and perceive the manner in which the air infiltrates your organism. Experience the expulsion of air from your respiratory system as you engage in the act of exhaling. Direct your attention to the manner in which your respiration alters as you place emphasis on the act of breathing. Develop an awareness of your ability to regulate your respiration and modify it according to your preferences.

Develop an Understanding of Your Emotional State

Devote a considerable period of time contemplating your sentiments or affective states. Please reflect upon the disparity between your present emotions and those experienced during earlier moments such as this morning or the preceding day. Employ a gentle approach in recollecting various emotions. Consider the range of emotions you commonly encounter, such as joy, anger, fear, sadness, excitement, and any other affective states that frequently manifest.

Develop an Understanding of Your Cognitive Processes

What thoughts are occupying your mind presently? Please make a mental record of your thoughts while you engage in reading this book or undertaking these exercises aimed at enhancing lucidity-comparison. Please bring your present thoughts to the forefront of your awareness and genuinely experience them. Occasionally, our mental constructs assume a sense of authenticity, whereas there are instances where the veracity of our thoughts may be subject to skepticism. Having an awareness of one's thoughts holds significant importance not just in the context of mindfulness, but also when it comes to the practice of lucid dreaming.

www.ingramcontent.com/pod-product-compliance
Lightning Source LLC
Chambersburg PA
CBHW050416120526
44590CB00015B/1980